DynamoDB Applied Design Patterns

Apply efficient DynamoDB design patterns for high performance of applications

Uchit Vyas

Prabhakaran Kuppusamy

BIRMINGHAM - MUMBAI

DynamoDB Applied Design Patterns

First published: September 2014

Production reference: 1160914

Published by Packt Publishing Ltd.
Livery Place
35 Livery Street
Birmingham B3 2PB, UK.

ISBN 978-1-78355-189-7

www.packtpub.com

Credits

Authors
Uchit Vyas
Prabhakaran Kuppusamy

Reviewers
Hrijul Parekh
Akshay Surve
Riddhi Thaker

Commissioning Editor
Pramila Balan

Acquisition Editor
Nikhil Karkal

Content Development Editor
Adrian Raposo

Technical Editor
Veronica Fernandes

Copy Editors
Roshni Banerjee
Sarang Chari

Project Coordinator
Sanchita Mandal

Proofreaders
Sam Birch
Paul Hindle

Indexer
Rekha Nair

Graphics
Disha Haria
Abhinash Sahu

Production Coordinator
Arvindkumar Gupta

Cover Work
Arvindkumar Gupta

About the Authors

Uchit Vyas is an open source specialist and a hands-on Lead DevOps of Clogeny Technologies. He is responsible for the delivery of solutions, services, and product development. He explores new open source technologies and defines architecture, roadmaps, and best practices for enterprises. He has consulted and provided training on various open source technologies, including Cloud computing (AWS Cloud, Rackspace, Azure, CloudStack, OpenStack, and Eucalyptus), Mule ESB, Chef, Puppet, Liferay Portal, Alfresco ECM, and JBoss to corporations around the world.

He has an engineering degree in Computer Science from Gujarat University. He was in the Education & Research Team as a senior associate at Infosys Limited, during which time he worked on SaaS, Private Clouds, Cloud Security, and Virtualization. He is now working on Cloud Automation.

He has also published a book on Mule ESB and is writing various books with Packt Publishing on open source technologies and AWS (*Mastering AWS Development Guide, Packt Publishing*).

He hosts a blog named Cloud Magic World (`cloudbyuchit.blogspot.com`), where he posts tips and phenomena about open source technologies, mostly relating to Cloud. He can also be found on twitter as `@uchit_vyas`.

I would like to thank my better half for helping me a lot in writing this book and providing me with continuous support all the time throughout the book-writing period. I would also like to thank my Infocian colleague, Prabhakaran Kuppusamy, for his great help.

Prabhakaran Kuppusamy is a Hadoop ecosystem specialist and Cloud enthusiast who is currently working as Senior Systems Engineer and developer, Cloud & Infrastructure Services unit, at Infosys Limited. He has been with Infosys for nearly 4 years now. He has a Bachelor of Engineering degree in Instrumentation and Control Engineering from Anna University. He joined Education & Research at Global Education Centre, Infosys, where he trained and evaluated thousands of freshers in Java, Big Data, and Cloud technologies. During his tenure in Education & Research, he provided training to students from Coventry University and to professionals from Costa Rica on Big Data and Cloud technologies, such as Hadoop, MapReduce, Hive, Elastic MapReduce, Google App Engine, DynamoDB, and CloudStack. It was during one of those training sessions that he met Uchit Vyas, and the idea of this book was born. After spending 2 years at the Global Education Centre, he moved to Cloud project management, where he started working on MarkLogic, Storm, and XQuery for a project on the banking domain. He can be found on Twitter at `@prabhakar28dec`.

Prabhakaran is currently working on the book *AWS Development Essentials, Packt Publishing*.

I would like to thank my mentors Sureesh Joseph, Bharathykannan Udhayasuriyan, Uchit Vyas, Bhupendra Bajpayi, and Ravindran Balachandran. Thanks for shepherding me personally and technically, by spending your time and goodwill in helping me spend valuable time on my maiden book and to bring the book out in good shape. Special thanks to Kshitiz Jain, my manager and friend, who has always been there to help me choose what suits me the best and helped me scale up in DynamoDB.

About the Reviewers

Hrijul Parekh has a B.Eng. degree in Information Technology with a research interest in Cloud and infrastructure automation. He is always enthusiastic to work on multiple platforms at a time and has the ability to integrate open source technologies. He is a Cloud Engineer at PMC Retail Pvt. Ltd.

With over 3 years of hands-on experience in open source technologies, he manages to guide the team and deliver projects and training sessions, meeting client expectations all along. He's responsible for designing and managing a Cloud environment/infrastructure and server architecture in his organization. He is also active in Shell scripting, autodeployment, supporting hundreds of Linux and Windows physical and virtual servers hosting databases, and applications with continuous delivery using Jenkins/Hudson with Chef scripting.

I would like to thank my family for supporting me to achieve my dreams.

Akshay Surve is in the pursuit of making meaning through his initiatives, be it for profit or for the good of society. At heart, he is a midnight code junkie and occasionally dabbles with prose.

He is also the cofounder and CTO at DeltaX, where he drives the technology and product roadmap. His expertise in Cloud computing and building web-scale distributed systems, coupled with a deep understanding of the ad-tech ecosystem over the last 8 years, has been one of the key drivers of the rapid pace of development of DeltaX's product line.

You can connect with him on Twitter. His Twitter handle is `@AkshaySurve`.

Riddhi Thaker has more than 4 years of software engineering experience in software design, analysis, development, testing, and implementation of web and client-server large-scale applications, as well as customized desktop applications based on Microsoft technologies and AWS infrastructure. She has extensive experience in design and development of applications using .NET and web technologies, such as XML, CSS, CSS3, Ajax, JavaScript, jQuery, UI designing, HTML, and HTML5 in *n*-tier architecture across platforms and even Cloud platforms.

She has a Bachelor's degree in Engineering in Information Technology from Gujarat University. She was in the Developer team as senior developer at BarodaWeb, during which time she worked on SaaS, private clouds, Azure, and virtualization. She is now working on Cloud deployment and various other Cloud platforms.

I would like to thank my better half for helping me a lot in reviewing this book and providing me with continuous support throughout the book reviewing period.

---

www.PacktPub.com

Support files, eBooks, discount offers, and more

You might want to visit www.PacktPub.com for support files and downloads related to your book.

Did you know that Packt offers eBook versions of every book published, with PDF and ePub files available? You can upgrade to the eBook version at www.PacktPub.com and as a print book customer, you are entitled to a discount on the eBook copy. Get in touch with us at service@packtpub.com for more details.

At www.PacktPub.com, you can also read a collection of free technical articles, sign up for a range of free newsletters and receive exclusive discounts and offers on Packt books and eBooks.

http://PacktLib.PacktPub.com

Do you need instant solutions to your IT questions? PacktLib is Packt's online digital book library. Here, you can access, read and search across Packt's entire library of books.

Why subscribe?

- Fully searchable across every book published by Packt
- Copy and paste, print and bookmark content
- On demand and accessible via web browser

Free access for Packt account holders

If you have an account with Packt at www.PacktPub.com, you can use this to access PacktLib today and view nine entirely free books. Simply use your login credentials for immediate access.

Table of Contents

Preface

This book, *DynamoDB Applied Design Patterns*, will be a single place to find solutions for all hiccups with Amazon DynamoDB. This book will explain how to create, design, and manage databases in DynamoDB using the AWS SDKs and APIs, as well as the AWS management console, a browser-based graphical user interface to interact with the service. It will include a significant number of examples that can be used by anyone, from a newbie to an expert. Using this book, users can perform advanced-level programming and gain the advantages of AWS DynamoDB NoSQL databases in their application at significantly lower costs.

What this book covers

Chapter 1, Data Modeling with DynamoDB, will teach users about data model concepts, including tables, items and attributes, primary key, and indexes and their design patterns.

Chapter 2, DynamoDB Interfaces, will help users gain knowledge of how to access DynamoDB in the management console. We will also take a look at the command-line interface and the Eclipse plugin.

Chapter 3, Tools and Libraries of AWS DynamoDB, will teach users what DynamoDB Local is, what the CLI commands are, and how we can use CLI from a developer/DBA perspective.

Chapter 4, Working with Secondary Indexes, will teach users what global and local secondary indexes are and what the importance of secondary indexes in DynamoDB is. Users will learn managed auto-sharding NoSQL databases that automatically reshard based on SLA.

Chapter 5, Query and Scan Operations in DynamoDB, will teach users about parallel scanning operations for DynamoDB. Users will learn how to use query and scan operations on DynamoDB tables and how to get results from query and scan operations.

Chapter 6, Working with the DynamoDB API, will take users through the Amazon DynamoDB API and its format. Users will learn how to call an API from applications to DynamoDB and how to retrieve data in an appropriate format that can be used with applications.

Chapter 7, Distributed Locking with DynamoDB, will provide readers with the information to support DynamoDB as an excellent choice for a distributed locking service, while briefly exploring the what, why, and how of locking.

Chapter 8, DynamoDB with Redshift, Data Pipeline, and MapReduce, will help readers work closely with DynamoDB from Redshift, S3, and MapReduce, and we will learn how to collaborate these AWS services with DynamoDB efficiently.

Chapter 9, DynamoDB – Best Practices, will help readers to deep dive into the best design use case architectures for DynamoDB. They will also learn real-time problem statements and their best solutions.

Appendix, Comparing DynamoDB, will teach users how Amazon DynamoDB is different than other NoSQL databases. So from that comparison, users will come to know the importance of DynamoDB while they are deploying their application with a NoSQL database.

What you need for this book

To start using this book, you need the following things:

- An AWS account
- JAVA 1.6 or higher
- Eclipse (Juno, Indigo, or Kepler)
- AWS SDK
- AWS CLI tools

Who this book is for

This book will be ideal for competent DynamoDB developers, architects, and DevOps. The reader should have a basic knowledge and understanding of AWS and different databases to allow efficient programming of core elements and applications with DynamoDB.

Conventions

In this book, you will find a number of styles of text that distinguish between different kinds of information. Here are some examples of these styles, and an explanation of their meaning.

Code words in text, database table names, folder names, filenames, file extensions, pathnames, dummy URLs, user input, and Twitter handles are shown as follows: "Therefore, during the creation of the `Tbl_Book` table in DynamoDB, we will specify only the `BookTitle` and `Author` attributes."

A block of code is set as follows:

```
aws dynamodb create-table --table-name Tbl_Book
--attribute-definitions AttributeName=BookTitle,AttributeType=S
  AttributeName=Author,AttributeType=S --key-schema
  AttributeName=BookTitle,KeyType=HASH
  AttributeName=Author,KeyType=RANGE
--provisioned-throughput ReadCapacityUnits=2,WriteCapacityUnits=2
```

When we wish to draw your attention to a particular part of a code block, the relevant lines or items are set in bold:

```
ScanRequest scanRequest = new ScanRequest()
  .withTableName("Tbl_Book");
ScanResult result = client.scan(scanRequest);
```

Any command-line input or output is written as follows:

```
copytable_uchitredshift from 'dynamodb:// table_uchitdynamodb'
credentials 'aws_access_key_id=xxxxx;aws_secret_access_key=xxx'
readratio 50;
```

New terms and **important words** are shown in bold. Words that you see on the screen, in menus or dialog boxes for example, appear in the text like this: "To view the inserted item, click on the **Browse Items** tab, select the **Scan** radio button, and click on the **Go** button."

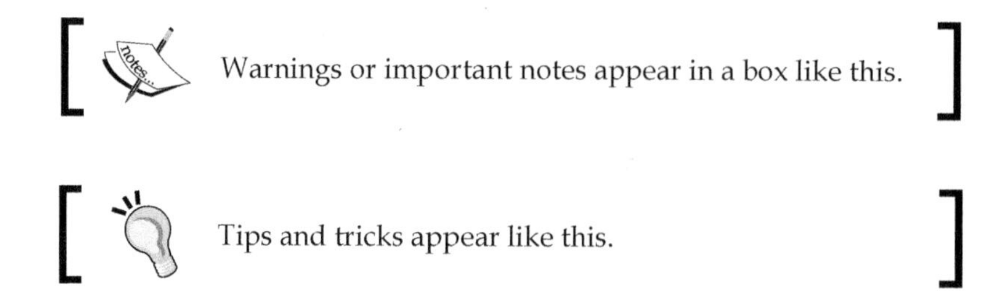

Reader feedback

Feedback from our readers is always welcome. Let us know what you think about this book—what you liked or may have disliked. Reader feedback is important for us to develop titles that you really get the most out of.

To send us general feedback, simply send an e-mail to `feedback@packtpub.com`, and mention the book title via the subject of your message.

If there is a topic that you have expertise in and you are interested in either writing or contributing to a book, see our author guide on `www.packtpub.com/authors`.

Customer support

Now that you are the proud owner of a Packt book, we have a number of things to help you to get the most from your purchase.

Errata

Although we have taken every care to ensure the accuracy of our content, mistakes do happen. If you find a mistake in one of our books—maybe a mistake in the text or the code—we would be grateful if you would report this to us. By doing so, you can save other readers from frustration and help us improve subsequent versions of this book. If you find any errata, please report them by visiting `http://www.packtpub.com/submit-errata`, selecting your book, clicking on the **errata submission form** link, and entering the details of your errata. Once your errata are verified, your submission will be accepted and the errata will be uploaded on our website, or added to any list of existing errata, under the Errata section of that title. Any existing errata can be viewed by selecting your title from `http://www.packtpub.com/support`.

Piracy

Piracy of copyright material on the Internet is an ongoing problem across all media. At Packt, we take the protection of our copyright and licenses very seriously. If you come across any illegal copies of our works, in any form, on the Internet, please provide us with the location address or website name immediately so that we can pursue a remedy.

Please contact us at `copyright@packtpub.com` with a link to the suspected pirated material.

We appreciate your help in protecting our authors, and our ability to bring you valuable content.

Questions

You can contact us at `questions@packtpub.com` if you are having a problem with any aspect of the book, and we will do our best to address it.

1

Data Modeling with DynamoDB

DynamoDB is a NoSQL database fully managed by Amazon, and it is made freely available (to a certain limit) as a web service. The meaning of *fully managed* is that all the patch installation, updates, data backup, replication, and all other security measures are taken care of by Amazon itself. Almost every NoSQL database has its own data model. A programmer or application designer always evaluates the strengths and weaknesses of a database by looking at its data model. This is the reason why we have taken DynamoDB data modeling for our primary discussion.

In this chapter we are going to discuss the basics of DynamoDB. The chapter is divided into four sections:

- Discussing DynamoDB data model concepts, such as tables, items, and attributes
- Continuing to discuss primary key creation and usage
- Using secondary indexes
- The different data types in DynamoDB

Data model

The following table makes understanding the data model easier. In RDBMS, a table is organized into rows and columns, but in DynamoDB we will never use these two words (except in this paragraph). Even if it is used mistakenly, please understand that rows are called items and columns are called attributes in DynamoDB, as shown in the following table:

RDBMS	DynamoDB
Row	Item
Column/field	Attribute

Table 1.0 – Data model

Having said that, let's go and look at realizing a table in DynamoDB. Throughout this book, we are going to use a common illustration. The common illustration is that of a library catalogue, and we are going to discuss examples related to it. Let's take a look at the library catalogue table:

Attribute	Data type	Attribute type	RDBMS type
BookTitle	String	Hash key	Compound primary key
Author	String	Range key	
Publisher	String	Optional attributes	Mandatory columns
PubDate	String		
Language	String		
Edition	Number		
Author2	String		

Table 1.1 – Library catalogue

If you wish to know how to create a table with the attributes mentioned in Table 1.1, read the *DynamoDB data types* section first. During the creation of a DynamoDB table, it is only possible to specify secondary index attributes, and hash and range key attributes. It is not possible to specify other attributes (previously mentioned as optional attributes) during the creation of the table. In fact, except for hash and range key attributes, all other attributes are part of the items (rows); that is the reason why we don't specify these optional attributes while creating the table.

Let's call the table Tbl_Book. The table has seven attributes. The first two attributes act as a compound primary key. We set the first attribute BookTitle as the hash key and the second attribute Author as the range key. Except for the primary key attributes, all other attributes are optional and we need not specify nonprimary key attributes while creating the table.

Therefore, during the creation of the Tbl_Book table in DynamoDB, we will specify only the BookTitle and Author attributes. All other attributes can be specified while inserting an item into this table.

Let's assume that Tbl_Book has been created in DynamoDB with BookTitle and Author attributes as the hash and range key. We will now insert four items into the table as shown:

Attribute	BookTitle	Author	Publisher	PubDate	Language	Edition	Author2
Item1	SCJP	Kathy	TMH		English	1	Bert Bates
Item2	Inferno	Dan Brown		14-May-13			
Item3	Let us C	Kanetkar			English		
Item4	SCJP	Khalid A M					Rolf W R
Item5	AWS	Prabhakaran	PACKT		English	1	

Table 1.2 – Tbl_Book

One quick question: while inserting the first item into the table, do we need to specify the PubDate attribute as null? The answer is no; every item can have its own attributes, along with mandatory primary key attributes specified during table creation. In fact, if we want to insert a fifth item with a new attribute named CoverPhoto, we can do it without affecting the previous four items.

Unlike RDBMS tables, the attributes (that is, what we call columns in RDBMS) of DynamoDB tables are stored in the item itself as a key-value pair. The attribute name becomes the key and the attribute value becomes the value. So every item will have its own attributes. There is a tradeoff here. Fetching a record will not only fetch the attribute value, but also its attribute name. So if you choose very long attribute names, then the efficiency will decrease.

Let's take a look at a few valid table schema that are supported by DynamoDB:

Attribute	Data type	Attribute type
BookTitle	String	Hash key
Authors	String	Range key
Editions	NumberSet	Optional attributes
CoverPhoto	Binary	

Table 1.3 – Valid schema

Attribute	Data type	Attribute type
BookTitle	String	Hash key
Authors	StringSet	Optional attributes
Editions	NumberSet	
CoverPhoto	Binary	

Table 1.4 – Valid schema

Attribute	Data type	Attribute type
BookTitle	String	Hash key

Table 1.5 – Valid schema

Attribute	Data type	Attribute type
BookTitle	String	Hash key
CoverPhoto	Binary	Range key

Table 1.6 – Valid schema

Let's take a look at a few invalid table schema:

Attribute	Data type	Attribute type
Authors	String	Range key
Editions	NumberSet	Optional attributes
CoverPhoto	Binary	

Table 1.7 – Invalid schema

Attribute	Data type	Attribute type
Authors	StringSet	Optional attributes
Editions	NumberSet	
CoverPhoto	Binary	

Table 1.8 – Invalid schema

Attribute	Data type	Attribute type
Authors	StringSet	Hash key
BookTitle	String	Range key

Table 1.9 – Invalid schema

Attribute	Data type	Attribute type
BookTitle	String	Hash key
Authors	NumberSet	Range key

Table 1.10 – Invalid schema

The schema for Table 1.7 is invalid, because it doesn't have the hash key attribute that is mandatory to create the table. Table 1.8 is invalid because of the same reason. The schemas for Table 1.9 and Table 1.10 are invalid because the hash and range keys must be either `String`, `Number`, or `Binary`. It cannot be `Set`. We will discuss the `Set` data type at the end of this chapter.

Once you have had a good look at a valid table schema, you will have the following questions for sure:

- What is the difference between the hash key and the range key?
- What is the difference between `String` data type and `StringSet` data type?
- Apart from `Set`, is there any other data type that I should know about?
- During table creation, what mandatory information should I provide?

Let us discuss the answers to these questions, which will help us understand the DynamoDB data model better. Here comes the answer to the first question. With the hash and range keys, hash and range are two attributes that act like a (compound) primary key. The range key must be accompanied by the hash key, but the hash key can optionally be accompanied by the range key. The hash key is an attribute that every table must have. It is an unordered collection of items; this means that items with the same hash key values will go to the same partition, but there won't be any ordering based on these hash key values, whereas items will always be ordered on range key values (but grouped on hash key values). After applying the previous statements to the already-created table, its order will look as follows:

BookTitle	**Author**	**Publisher**	**PubDate**	**Language**	**Language2**	**Edition**	**Author2**
SCJP	Kathy	TMH		English	English	1	Bert Bates
SCJP	Khalid A M						Rolf W R
Let us C	Kanetkar			English	English		
Inferno	Dan Brown		14-May-13				

Table 1.11 – Hash Key values

So there is no guarantee that the table data will be sorted by the hash key (that is `BookTitle`), but it will be hashed or grouped based on the hash key attribute value. That is the reason why `Item1` and `Item4` are placed close together. On the other hand, the records are ordered on the range key (that is, `Author`). That is the reason why the book SCJP authored by Kathy is first, followed by the book authored by Khalid. This answers the first question.

An attribute of the type `String` can hold only a simple string. For example, in the previous table we have two attributes (`Language` and `Language2`) to store the edition language of the book. If a book has 10 different language editions, then we would be left with too many attributes in an item (which will reduce fetch efficiency as discussed on the previous page). So a better solution is to change the `Language` attribute from a simple `String` type to `StringSet` as shown in the following table:

Attribute	BookTitle	Author	Publisher	PubDate	Language	Edition	Author2
Item1	SCJP	Kathy	TMH		{"English", "German"}	1	Bert Bates
Item4	SCJP	Khalid A M			{"English"}		Rolf W R
Item3	Let us C	Kanetkar			{"English"}		
Item2	Inferno	Dan Brown		14-May-13	{"English"}		

Table 1.12 – String attribute

The same cannot be done for the `Author` attribute. Can you guess why? If not, you can go back and take a look at Table 1.9 and Table 1.10. Can you guess now? It's because neither the hash key nor the range key can be of the `Set` type.

At present there are only six data types in DynamoDB, namely `String`, `Number`, `Binary`, `StringSet`, `NumberSet`, and `BinarySet`. We will discuss this at the end of this chapter.

During table creation, there are two scenarios that decide the mandatory parameters needed to create a DynamoDB table.

- **Hash primary key**: In this scenario we must (and we can only) provide two parameters. The first parameter is the table name, and the second parameter is the name and type of hash key.
- **Hash and range primary key**: In this scenario, we must (and we can only) provide three parameters. The first parameter is the table name, the second parameter is the name and type of hash key, and the third parameter is the name and type of range key.

There are different interfaces available to interact with DynamoDB. Take a look at *Chapter 2, DynamoDB Interfaces*, to know more about the interfaces. We are now done with the basics of this chapter.

Efficient use of primary keys

As DynamoDB is a NoSQL database and is used with scalable applications, table data might grow exponentially. This might reduce data read and write throughput (the number of 1 KB read or write requests per second) if not managed efficiently. This management starts right from choosing the correct primary key and its parameters. Take a look at the following table:

BookTitle	Author	Publisher	PubDate	Language	Edition	Author2
SCJP	Kathy	TMH		{"English", "German"}	1	Bert Bates
SCJP	Khalid A M			{"English"}		Rolf W R
Let us C	Kanetkar			{"English"}		
Inferno	Dan Brown		14-May-13	{"English"}		

Table 1.13 – Primary key

As soon as the table is created, the table data is partitioned on the hash key attribute. What this means is that if the table has three partitions, then the first two items will go to the first partition, the third item will go to the second partition and the last item will go to the third partition. This partition is based purely on hash logic, which we are not going to discuss here.

In our library catalogue example, we are always looking for a certain book, with the assumption that the first thing that comes to our mind when identifying a book is its title. That is why we decided to set the `BookTitle` attribute as the hash key. Another reason why we chose this specific attribute as the hash key is the assumption that most of the scan operations for the table will include the `BookTitle` attribute.

DynamoDB does not allow duplication of the hash key (provided that the table does not have a range attribute), so if the primary key is a simple hash key, then we are enforcing that an entry cannot be made into the previous table with the same book title. But in a real-world scenario this is not the case. So we are in need of a range key attribute as well. The next decision to be taken is what should be made the range attribute. We will assume that the second attribute that comes to mind when identifying a book is the name of its author. Unlike the hash key attribute, range key attributes are ordered (also grouped on the hash key attribute). Here also we are enforcing upon DynamoDB that the same author will never write a book on the same title.

Take a look at the following table (which is **incorrect** and is shown only to understand the concept):

BookTitle	Author	Publisher	PubDate	Language	Edition	Author2
SCJP	Kathy	TMH		{"English", "German"}	1	Bert Bates
SCJP	**Kathy**	TMH		{"German"}	3	Bert Bates
SCJP	Khalid A M			{"English"}		Rolf W R
Let us C	Kanetkar			{"English"}		
Inferno	Dan Brown		14-May-13	{"English"}		

Table 1.14 – Duplication of hash key

But this might fail in several cases because the later editions of the book might have been authored by the same author. In this case, the second item insertion will simply overwrite the first item because the primary key is duplicated. As a solution, at this point in time I'd recommend you to concatenate the `Author` attribute along with the `Edition` attribute separated by `#` (or any other acceptable delimiter). So the table will look as follows:

BookTitle	Author#Edition	Publisher	PubDate	Language	Author2
SCJP	**Kathy#1**	TMH		{"English", "German"}	Bert Bates
SCJP	**Kathy#3**	TMH		{"German"}	Bert Bates
SCJP	Khalid A M			{"English"}	Rolf W R
Let us C	Kanetkar			{"English"}	
Inferno	Dan Brown		14-May-13	{"English"}	

Table 1.15 – Concatenate

Observe the `String` range key attribute `Author#Edition`. Even if some of the items don't have the edition included in the range key attribute, it will not create any trouble at the DynamoDB end (but we have to take care from the application programming front).

Some of you might have thought of making the range key attribute type as `StringSet`, but remember that hash or range key attributes cannot be a `Set` type.

There are a few things to be kept in mind before choosing the correct hash and range attributes:

- Since the table is partitioned based on the hash key attribute, do not choose repeating attributes that will have only single-digit (very few) unique values. For example, the `Language` attribute of our table has only three identical values. Choosing this attribute will eat up a lot of throughput.
- Give the most restricted data type. For example, if we decide to make some number attributes as primary key attributes, then (even though `String` can also store numbers) we must use the `Number` data type only, because the hash and ordering logic will differ for each data type. Other advantages will be discussed in *Chapter 5, Query and Scan Operations in DynamoDB*, while discussing query and scan.
- Do not put too many attributes or too lengthy attributes (using delimiter as discussed formerly) into the primary key attributes, because it becomes mandatory that every item must have these attributes and all the attributes will become part of the query operation, which is inefficient.
- Make the attribute to be ordered as the range key attribute.
- Make the attribute to be grouped (or partitioned) as the hash key attribute.

Basics of indexes

Just imagine that we are entering a hypermarket to purchase a few grocery items, which we have already noted on a piece of paper. It's a multistorey store. Being a hypermarket, it has almost all the products, such as grocery items, home appliances, electronics, footwear, and lifestyle items. Since our intention is to purchase grocery items, we start with olive oil, and we find it located on the first floor, but the cookware is not available on the same floor; it's available on the top floor (let's say the tenth floor). After dragging ourselves from the bottom floor to the top floor, we find that we were especially looking to buy a microwave oven, but guess what? It is available on the fifth floor. So we are thinking of getting the elevator and going to the fifth floor. In spite of the badly-arranged items (not only with grocery items), almost all the people are using the elevator, because of which we couldn't purchase the microwave oven (along with some other items). So it's a loss of money for the store as well as a waste of time for the customers.

We are entering another hypermarket, that has all the grocery items placed on the first floor. Along with the items noted on the paper, we are purchasing a few more items that we missed out while writing. In this way both the customer and the store will benefit. Which store will you choose to shop in the next time? If you say that I love the first store and I will always choose to purchase items only from that store, then please read *Chapter 4, Working with Secondary Indexes*, which covers the usage of secondary index.

So you can call a store or hypermarket perfectly managed only if it helps the customer complete his/her purchase easily. This can be done by organizing the items properly. Similarly you can call a database properly managed only if the elements or items are organized in such a way that it allows easy and fast retrieval of items in the table (in NoSQL, we don't care much about insertion speed, since the data is read multiple times when it is written or updated).

Indexes make retrieval much faster and minimize your billing in many ways. We are going to discuss a few secondary index basics here, and a much more detailed discussion will continue in *Chapter 4, Working with Secondary Indexes*.

Default or primary indexes

Do you know that whenever you create a DynamoDB table, an index is also created? That index is called as primary index. This primary index will include the primary key attributes (both hash and range keys). The index created over a hash key is an unordered hash index. What it means is that the items with the same hash key will be grouped together and placed adjacent to each other, which helps in faster retrieval of items with the same hash key attributes (using the scan operation), but there will not be any ordering in the item on the hash key attribute.

Just for illustration purposes, let's go back to the `Tbl_Book` table:

BookTitle	Author#Edition	Publisher	PubDate	Language	Author2
SCJP	Kathy#1	TMH		{"English", "German"}	Bert Bates
SCJP	Kathy#3	TMH		{"German"}	Bert Bates
SCJP	Khalid#7			{"English"}	Rolf W R
Let us C	Kanetkar			{"English"}	
Inferno	Dan Brown		14-May-13	{"English"}	

Table 1.16 –Tbl_Book

Here, you can see that the items with the same `BookTitle` attribute (which is the hash key attribute) are placed adjacent to each other, because as soon as the table is created, this index will be created, and whenever an insertion takes place it will hash this attribute using some hash logic and place it in the correct location. If you look at the ASCII code or the English alphabetical order, *L* as in *Let us C* comes before *S* as in *SCJP*. Since the index created on the hash key is unordered, the items will not be sorted on this attribute.

Another noticeable concept is the index created on the `Author#Edition` attribute (which is the range key attribute); it works deeper on the tree created by the hash key index. This index will order the items that have the same hash key (but of course with different range key values) either in descending or ascending order. To put it in RDBMS terms, the hash key index will perform `GROUP BY` and the range key index will perform the `ORDER BY` action.

Secondary indexes

Primary indexes are created by DynamoDB by default. Along with those indexes, the user can create up to five secondary indexes for a table. There are two kinds of secondary indexes:

- The first is the local secondary index (in which the hash key of the index must be the same as that of the table)
- The second is the global secondary index (in which the hash key can be any field)

In both of these secondary index types, the range key can be a field, which the user needs to create the index for.

In the case of the local secondary index, the grouping will always take place on the hash key attribute, whereas the ordering takes place on the nonprimary key attribute. A quick question: in DynamoDB, except for primary key attributes, all other attributes are optional for an item. So where do these index attributes fall, in optional attributes or mandatory attributes? The answer is that local secondary index attributes are also optional attributes. If an item does not include this attribute, then that item will not be indexed, it's as simple as that.

We will take a look at an example in the following table:

BookTitle	Author#Edition	Publisher	PubDate	Language	Author2
SCJP	Kathy#1	TMH	28-Dec-09	{"English", "German"}	Bert Bates
SCJP	Kathy#3	TMH	14-Mar-09	{"German"}	Bert Bates
SCJP	Khalid#7			{"English"}	Rolf W R
Let us C	Kanetkar		13-Apr-10	{"English"}	
Inferno	Dan Brown		14-May-13	{"English"}	

Table 1.17 – Secondary index

Let's say that we are creating a local secondary index on the `PubDate` attribute. Let's name this index `Idx_PubDate`. The index will look as shown in the next table. This is the smallest local secondary index we can create (we are not going to discuss projections yet. We will discuss them in *Chapter 4, Working with Secondary Indexes*). Take a look at the following table:

BookTitle	PubDate
SCJP	14-Mar-09
SCJP	28-Dec-09
Let us C	13-Apr-10
Inferno	14-May-13

Table 1.18 – Local secondary index

You will quickly notice that the third item did not have the secondary index attribute, so that item is not available in the index. One more change is that the index is sorted on the `PubDate` attribute, so the first item became the second item.

In the case of the local secondary index, there is a restriction that the hash key of the table must be the hash key of the index too. In order to overcome this, we can also specify the user-defined (non-primary key attribute) attribute as the hash key attribute of the secondary index. Then this index will be called the global secondary index.

Let's take a scenario in which we need to count the number of unique languages a publisher has published the book in. In this case, the publisher name will become the `GROUP BY` column (index hash key) and the Language column will become the `ORDER BY` column (index range key). Take a look at the following tables:

BookTitle	Author#Ed	Publisher	PubDate	Language
SCJP	Kathy#1	TMH	28-Dec-09	"English"
SCJP	Kathy#3	TMH	14-Mar-09	"German"
SCJP	Khalid#7	Wiley India		"English"
Let us C	Kanetkar		13-Apr-10	"English"
Inferno	Dan Brown	Double Day	14-May-13	

Table 1.19 – Index hash key

Publisher	Language
TMH	"English"
TMH	"German"
Wiley India	"English"

Table 1.20 – Index range key

In this case, the item will be put into the index only if both the attributes of the index are available in the item. That is the reason why two items are not available in the global secondary index.

DynamoDB data types

DynamoDB supports six data types, namely `String`, `Number`, `Binary`, `StringSet`, `NumberSet`, and `BinarySet`. To understand this better, we will get some help from the AWS management console. Once we have signed up with AWS, our management console will look for an icon to work with DynamoDB, as shown in the following screenshot:

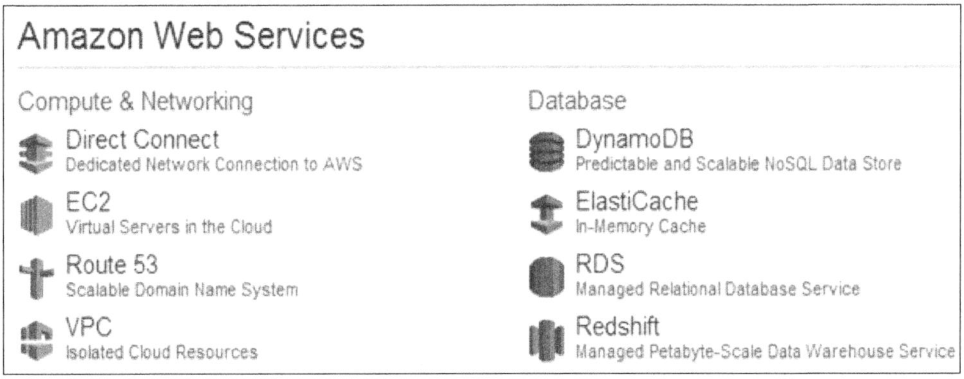

Amazon Web Services

Compute & Networking

Direct Connect
Dedicated Network Connection to AWS

EC2
Virtual Servers in the Cloud

Route 53
Scalable Domain Name System

VPC
Isolated Cloud Resources

Database

DynamoDB
Predictable and Scalable NoSQL Data Store

ElastiCache
In-Memory Cache

RDS
Managed Relational Database Service

Redshift
Managed Petabyte-Scale Data Warehouse Service

Clicking on the DynamoDB icon for the first time will take us to a getting started page, which has guidelines on starting with DynamoDB. We should click on the **Create Table** button to create our first table. We are now going to create the `Tbl_Book` table, which we have seen enough times. We are also going to insert only one item into this table. The table and its item are as shown:

BookTitle	Author	Publisher	PubDate	Language	Edition
String (hash)	String (range)	String	String	StringSet	Number
SCJP	Kathy	TMH	28-Dec-09	{"English", "German"}	1

Table 1.21 – Tbl_Book

After clicking on **Create Table**, you will see the following page. Here you have to provide **Table Name**, **Hash Attribute Name**, and **Range Attribute Name**. After providing the necessary parameters, you can proceed further.

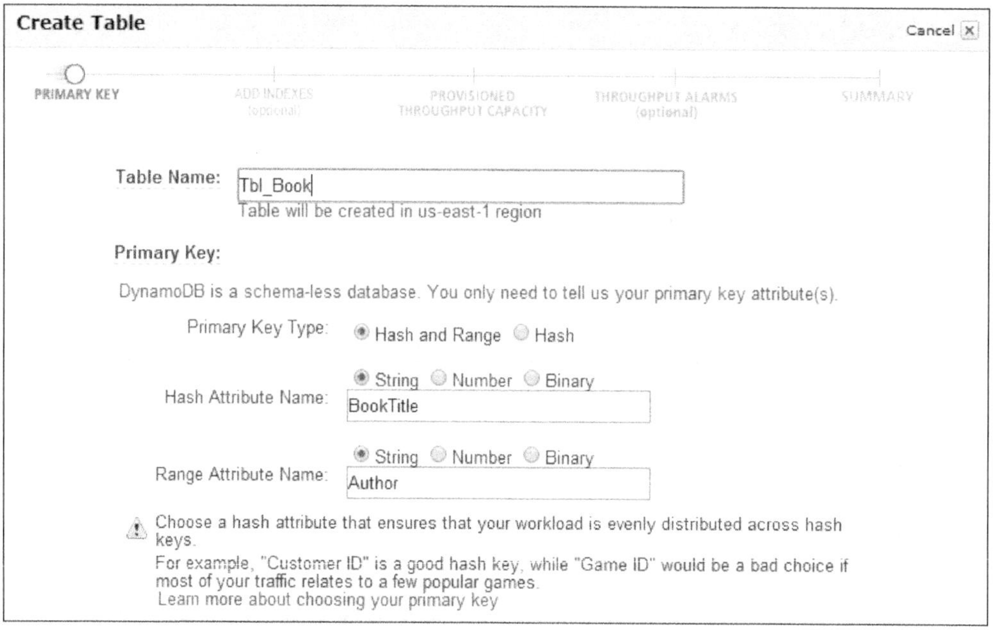

Create Table Cancel

PRIMARY KEY | ADD INDEXES (optional) | PROVISIONED THROUGHPUT CAPACITY | THROUGHPUT ALARMS (optional) | SUMMARY

Table Name: Tbl_Book
Table will be created in us-east-1 region

Primary Key:

DynamoDB is a schema-less database. You only need to tell us your primary key attribute(s).

Primary Key Type: (•) Hash and Range ( ) Hash

Hash Attribute Name: (•) String ( ) Number ( ) Binary — BookTitle

Range Attribute Name: (•) String ( ) Number ( ) Binary — Author

Choose a hash attribute that ensures that your workload is evenly distributed across hash keys.
For example, "Customer ID" is a good hash key, while "Game ID" would be a bad choice if most of your traffic relates to a few popular games.
Learn more about choosing your primary key

As we discussed, during the creation of the table we need to specify only the primary key attributes along with the table name. In this table, both the key elements are of type `String`.

If we need to create a simple hash (without range key) primary key, then we can select the **Hash** radio button instead of **Hash and Range**.

The next page will provide an option to create secondary indexes, which we need not bother about now. Once we proceed with all the command buttons in the browser, we will see the page in the following screenshot:

Initially, the status will be **CREATING**. Once it becomes **ACTIVE**, we can click on **Explore Table** (as shown in the previous screenshot) to insert (or scan) items into the table.

Once we have clicked on **Explore Table**, we should again click on the **New Item** button to insert an item. Clicking on this button will open the window in the following screenshot (we have already populated it to save paper):

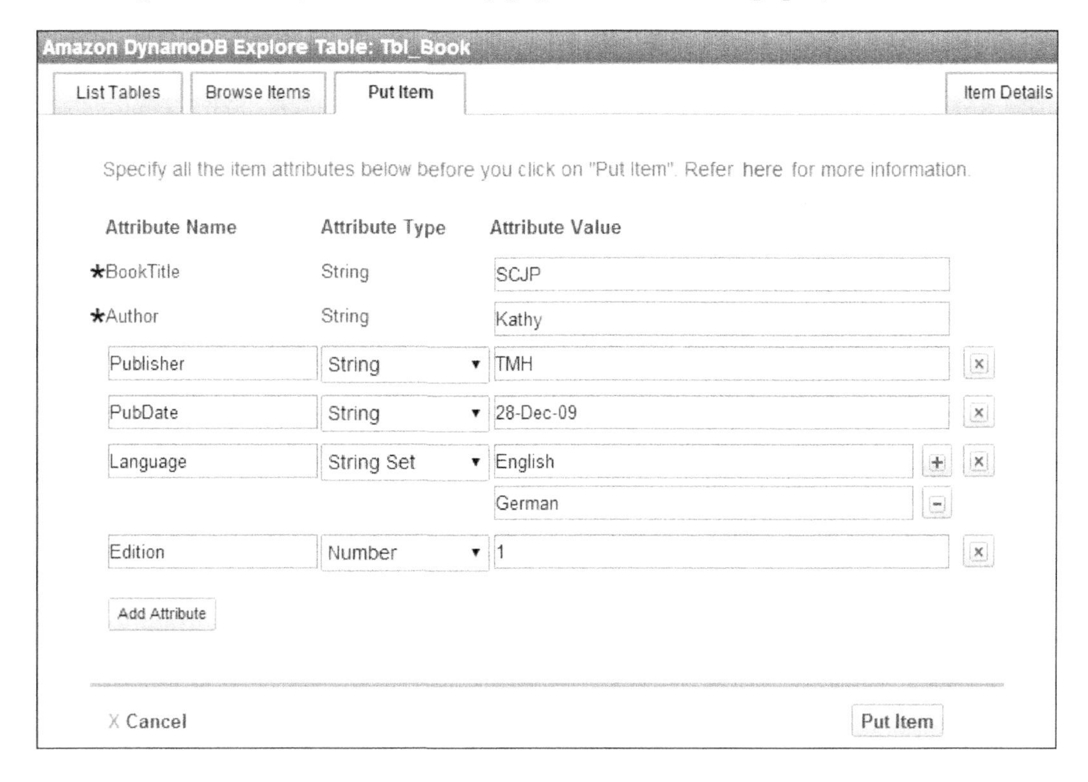

The mandatory attributes, name and type, will be already populated and we cannot change them. But we can add the attribute values (which must be unique).

In addition to that, we can simple click on empty textboxes (under hash and range key attribute name) to add item-specific attribute name, type, and value.

Here the first four attributes are of the type `String`, so we can enter the corresponding values in the attribute value field.

While entering multivalued data for a `Set` data type (`StringSet` for the **Language** field), specify multiple strings or numbers by clicking on the plus sign to the right of the value textbox. Once all the attributes are entered, click on the **Put Item** button, which will put this item into the `Tbl_Book` table.

To view the inserted item, click on the **Browse Items** tab, select the **Scan** radio button, and click on the **Go** button. Now we will be able to see the table content as shown in the following screenshot:

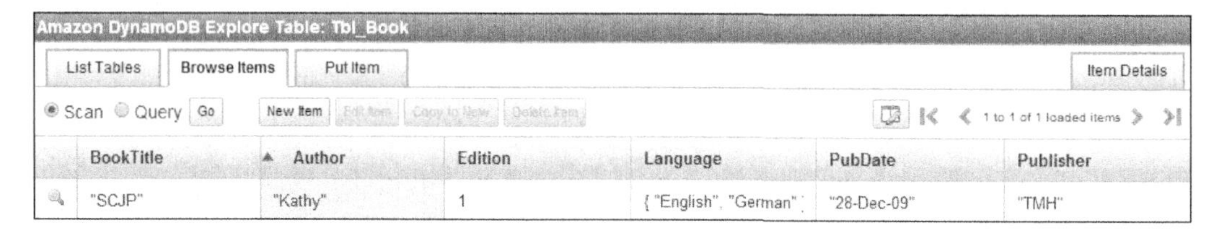

The `String` attribute values are enclosed in double quotes, and the `Set` attribute values are enclosed by set brackets. The number attribute values won't be enclosed by any character.

There are a few rules while using the `Set` data type. These rules are as follows:

- `Set` must have a nonzero number of elements (that is, empty sets are not permitted)
- `Set` must not have duplicate values (that is, the `Language` set will not take `English`, `English`)

There is a special kind of data type, called `Binary`, which is capable of storing Base64 encoded values. It is also used to store images or pictures in the Base64 encoded format. We will see it in *Chapter 6, Working with the DynamoDB API*.

Summary

In this chapter, we learned about data model concepts, including tables, items and attributes, primary key, and indexes and their design patterns.

We started the chapter by discussing the DynamoDB data model where we understood the importance of primary keys. We then took a look at a few valid and invalid table schema. We understood the basic significance of DynamoDB indexes. Finally, there was some explanation of the DynamoDB data types that we have used so far in the chapter. This is a basic chapter and we are going to cover similar topics in the upcoming chapters in greater detail.

In this chapter we took a look at the AWS management console. But along with the management console we can interact with DynamoDB in numerous ways, which we are going to see in the next chapter along with the installation and configuration details. We will learn how to access DynamoDB in the management console, command line, and the Eclipse plugin.

2

DynamoDB Interfaces

There are a number of interfaces available to make user interaction easy and effective. There are four interfaces that are commonly used to interact with DynamoDB:

- The management console
- The Eclipse plugin
- The command-line interface
- The REST API

As a part of our discussion in this chapter, we will learn about the first three interfaces. We will discuss the fourth interface in detail in *Chapter 6, Working with the DynamoDB API*.

The management console

The management console is one of the most commonly used interfaces in DynamoDB because of its simplicity of use. There is another reason that the end user will prefer the management console: it doesn't require any software to start with. Just having an Internet connection and a browser is sufficient.

Once you sign up with AWS, just click on **Management Console**. This will take you to the following page:

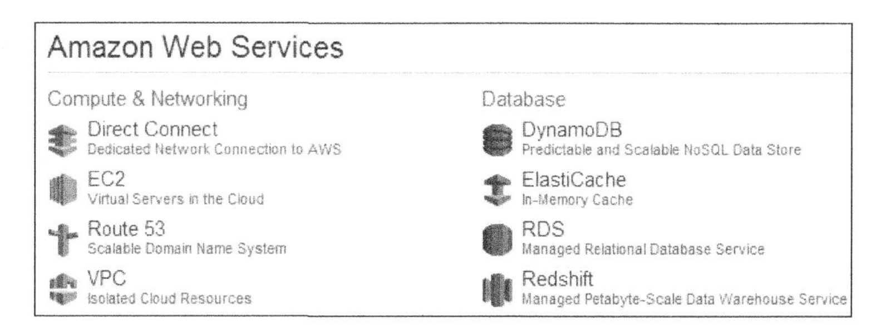

The **DynamoDB** option is available in the **Database** section of the management console. We can click on this icon to begin DynamoDB. We will divide this section into two parts. Initially we will discuss how to manage a table and then we will discuss how to manage items using the management console.

Managing the DynamoDB table

Clicking on **DynamoDB** in the management console for the first time will open a page that consists of three sections:

- The first section in the top-left corner provides information such as where the tables will be created (this can be changed by clicking in the top-right corner of the page, where **N. California** is currently) and a button to create a DynamoDB table.
- The second section in the bottom-left corner displays the steps involved in table creation.
- The third section on the right-hand side provides additional links to get further information about DynamoDB. This section consists of a video depicting the advantages of DynamoDB.

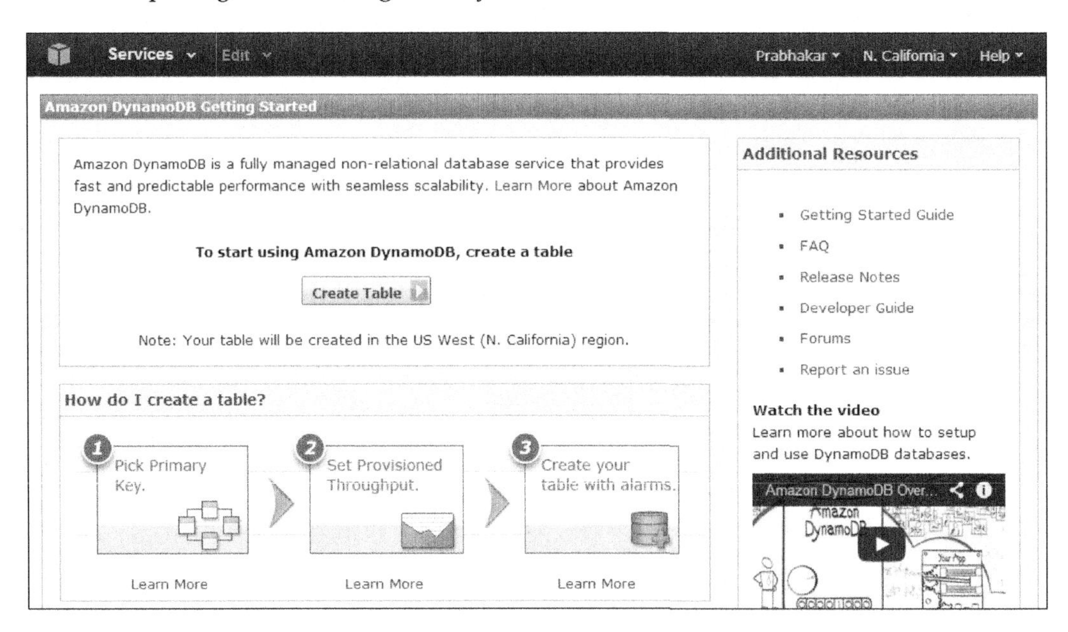

Clicking on the **Create Table** button will open the following page that asks for mandatory table creation parameters, that is **Table Name** and the **Primary Key** attribute names and type:

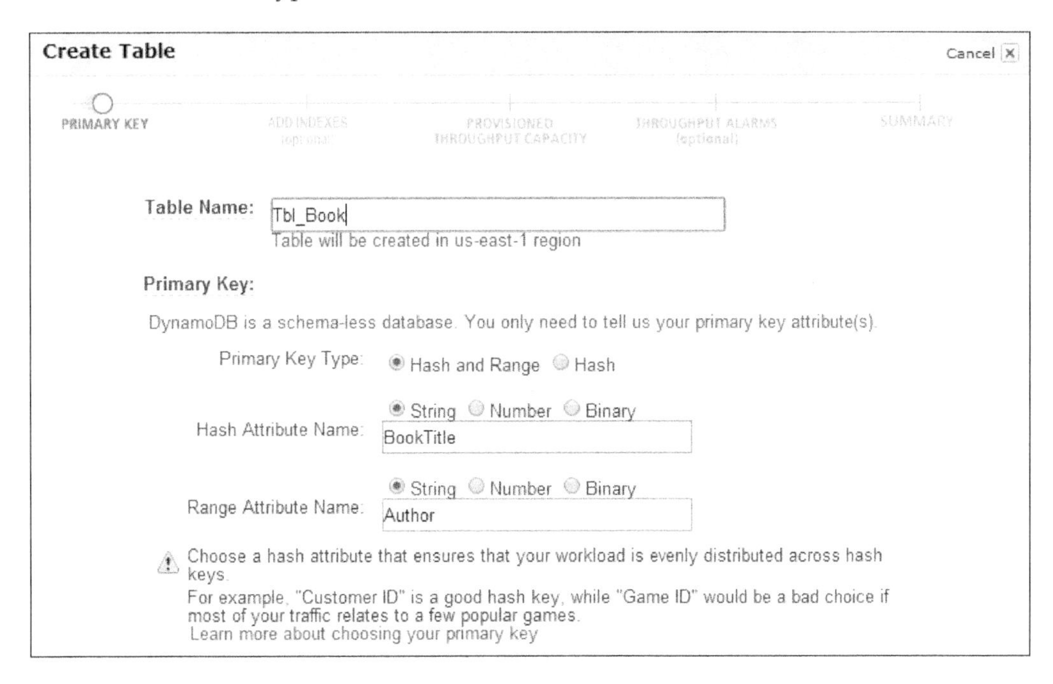

After clicking on the **Continue** button, the **Add Indexes** page will appear. Since DynamoDB doesn't allow us to create indexes after table creation, we must specify the indexes during table creation itself.

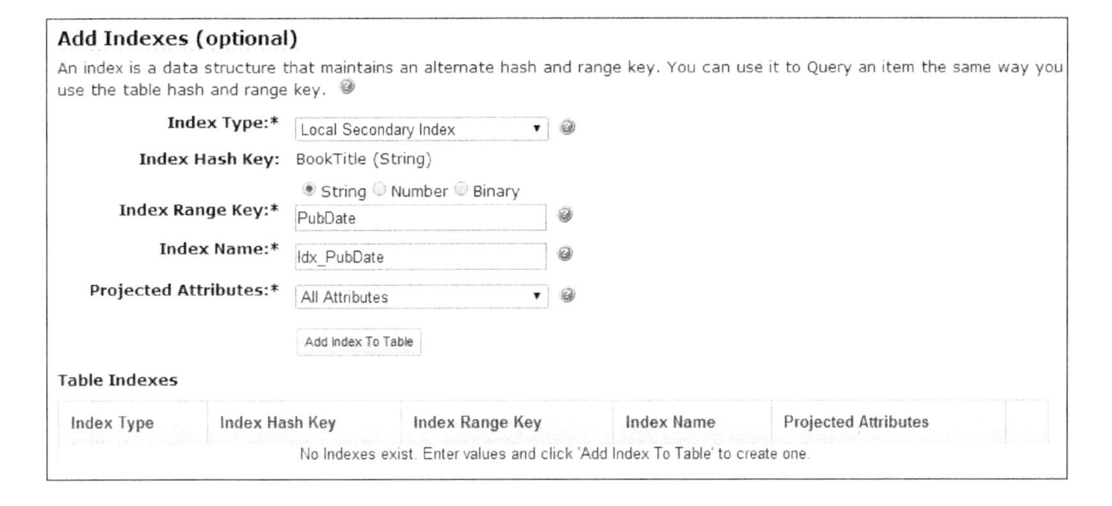

We can select the type of secondary index (local or global) by providing the necessary parameters as shown earlier. Clicking on the **Add Index To Table** button will validate and add the index to the table, and will be listed. A warning message will be displayed stating that it is not possible to add an index once the table is created.

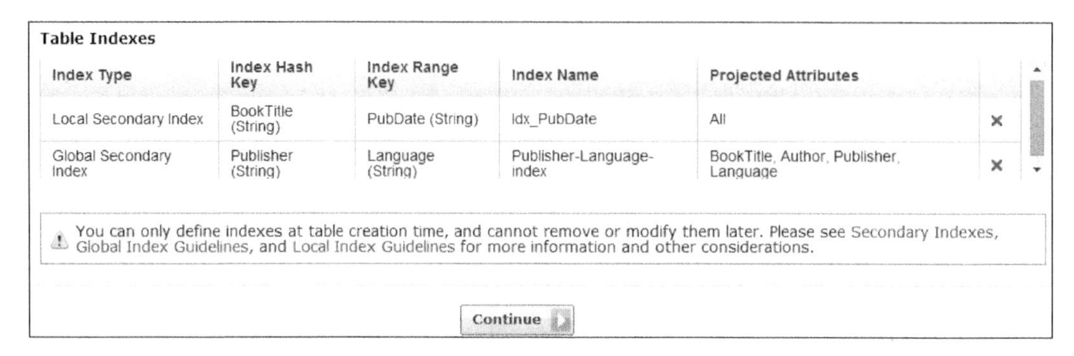

The next page will allow us to specify the read/write speed from our DynamoDB table. The value we specify here will be divided among the indexes too. The good news is that even after creating the table we can change this provision throughput value at any point in time. A detailed explanation about performance dependency on provisional throughput is covered in *Chapter 4, Working with Secondary Indexes*, and *Chapter 5, Query and Scan Operations in DynamoDB*.

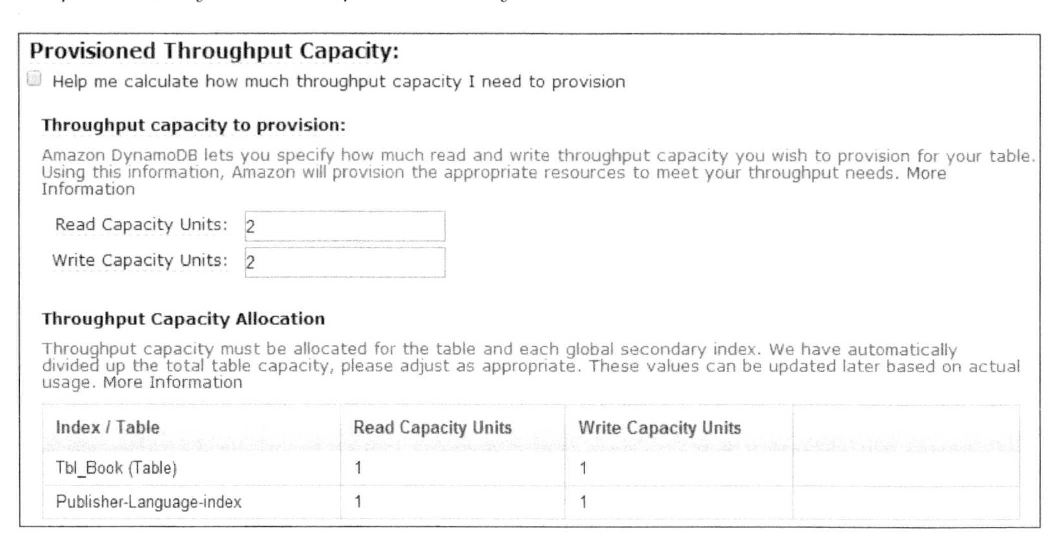

The following page will create an alarm for the table's throughput capacity. We can specify the e-mail ID and threshold value. If the read or write requests directed to the table exceed the specified value (in the following screenshot, the threshold is **80%**) then a mail intimation will be sent. This is completely optional; however, to avoid billing it's better to disable this by not using any alarms.

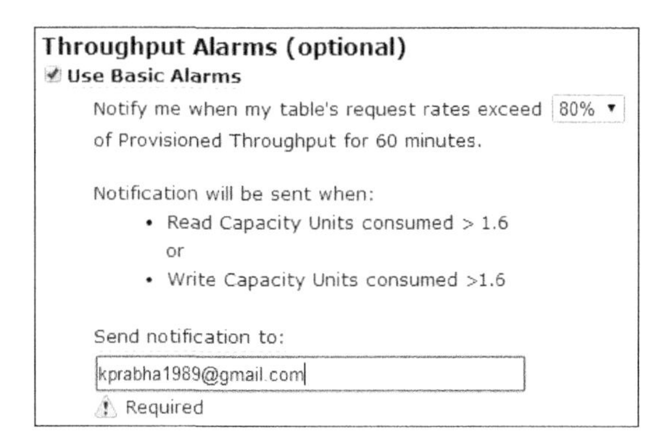

The following summary page displays all the table configurations we have specified so far. Just confirm and click on the **Create** button. Otherwise, we can go back and change the configuration using the **Back** button.

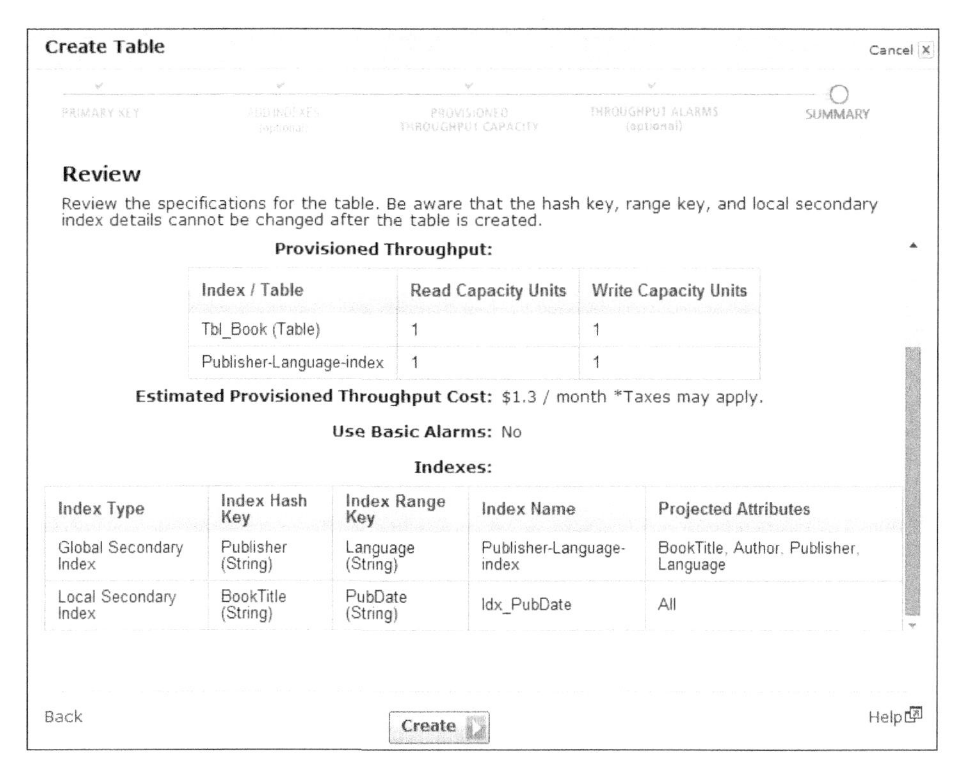

Clicking on the **Create** button will take us to the following page, with the table status **CREATING**:

In a couple of minutes, the status of the table will change to **ACTIVE** and clicking on the table name will show additional details about the table.

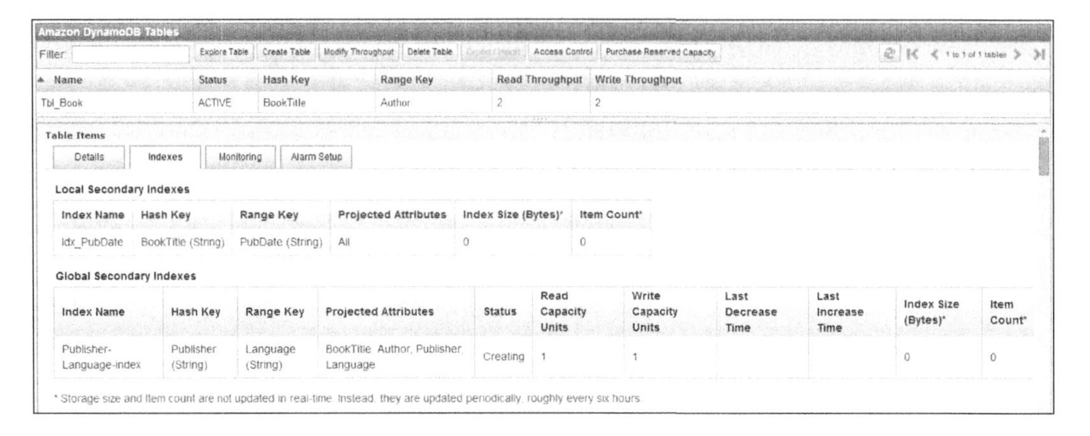

Managing DynamoDB table items

In order to add items to the DynamoDB table, select the table and click on the **Explore Table** button. It will open the following page, which allows us to enter the item details. Once done, click on **Put Item** to add the item.

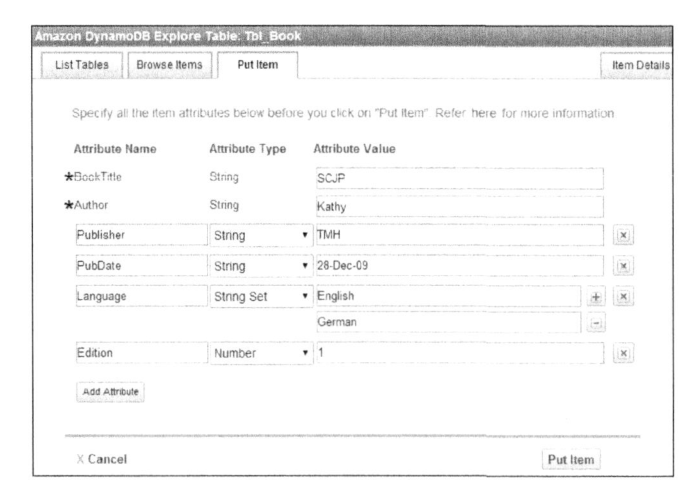

In order to scan the entire DynamoDB table, select the **Browse Items** tab, select the **Scan** radio button, and click on the **Go** button. It will display all the items entered into this table.

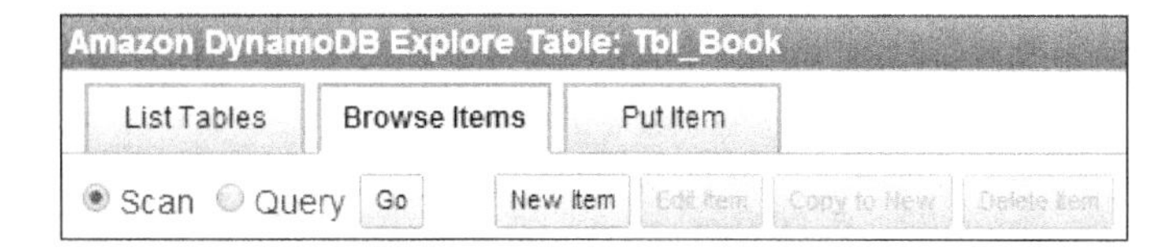

The **Scan** radio button will not allow us to specify the condition for retrieving items, but **Query** will allow us to do that. Clicking on the **Go** button after selecting the **Query** radio button will show all the indexes for the selected table. Selecting the index from the dropdown will automatically update the **Hash Key** and **Range Key** dropdowns (as shown in the following screenshots). The first index is the primary index and the rest are secondary.

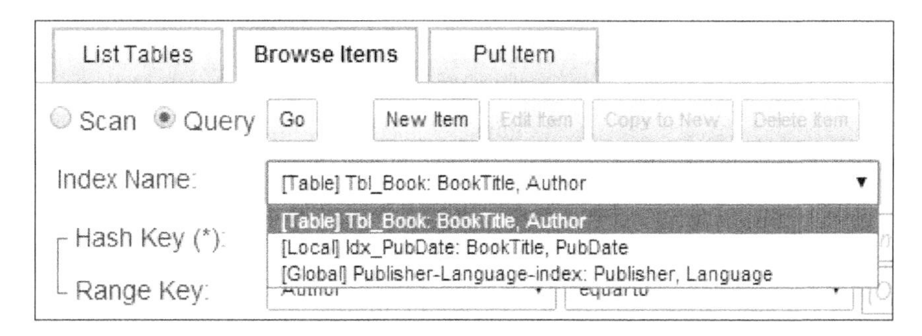

There are only two **Hash Key** attributes (**BookTitle** and **Publisher**) involved in the three indexes.

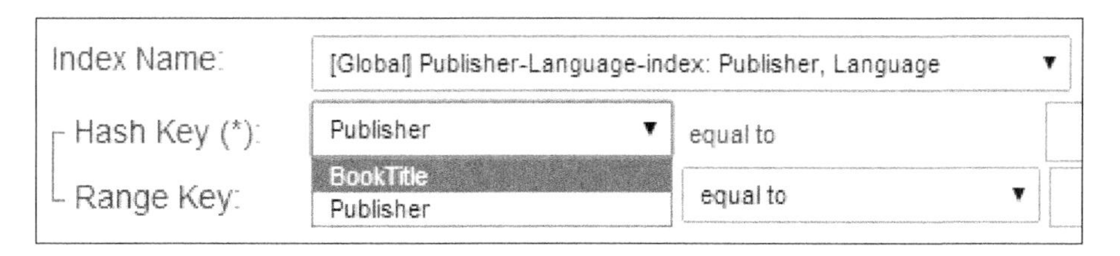

Selecting the **BookTitle** attribute as **Hash Key** will populate the necessary **Range Key** attributes. Can you guess why the **Language** range key is not populated? It's because **Language** is the range key of the global secondary index, with hash key as **Publisher**. Since the **Publisher** hash key is not selected (and **BookTitle** is selected), the **Language** attribute is not loaded.

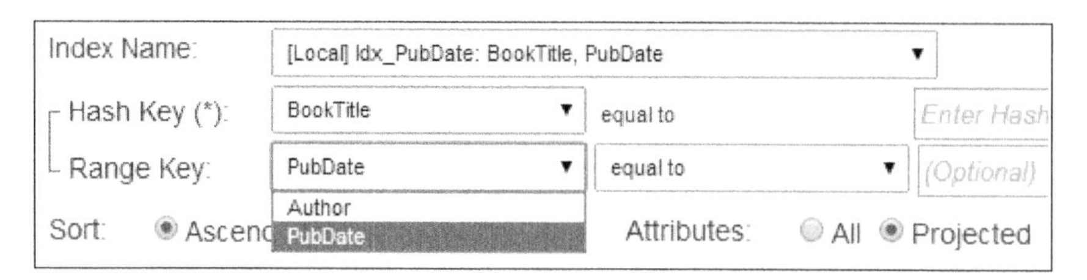

Additionally we can specify whether the query should return only the projected attributes or all the attributes of the index using the **Attributes** radio button, as shown in the previous screenshot.

Selecting **Publisher** from the **Hash Key** dropdown will populate only the **Language** attribute in the **Range Key** dropdown. This is because **Publisher** is a hash key only in the global index, whereas in the local index and table index **BookTitle** is the hash key. This is the rule of thumb.

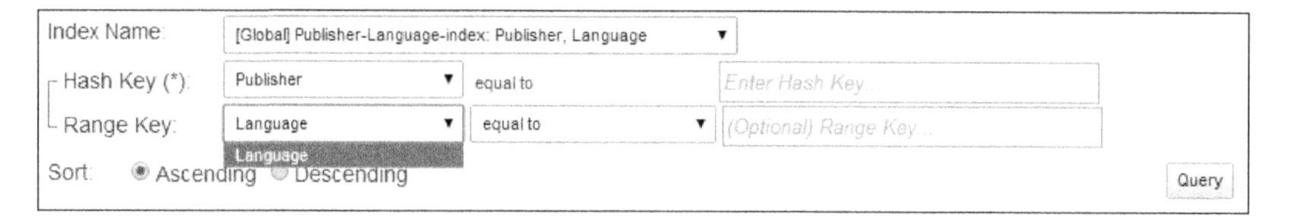

It is also possible for us to specify the sorting order of the query result by using the **Sort** radio button, as shown in the previous screenshot. Clicking on the **Query** radio button will fetch us the result.

As soon as the result is displayed and if we select an item, the following options will appear to work on the item. The first button, **New Item**, will help us to put an item into the table. The second button, **Edit Item**, will allow us to modify or update the existing item. The third button, **Copy to New**, will allow us to create a new item from the selected item, but with different primary key. The last button, **Delete Item**, will remove the item from the table.

The Eclipse plugin

Eclipse, being one of the most commonly-used open source **integrated development environments (IDEs)**, provides a plugin to work with DynamoDB. In fact it provides a plugin to work with almost the entire AWS. We will now see how to perform DynamoDB operations such as table creation, index creation, items insertion, and query and scan operations.

First we will begin with setting up the DynamoDB plugin on Eclipse. Open Eclipse and select **Install New Software** from the **Help** menu.

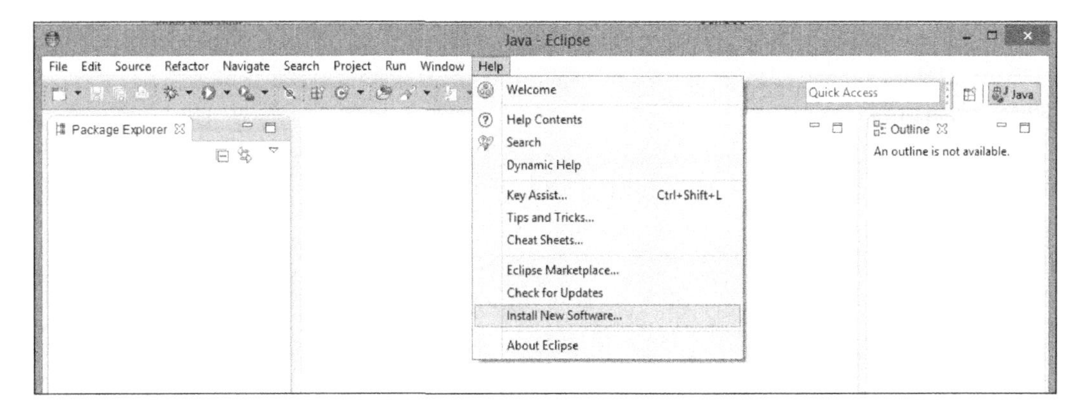

In the following page, we need to enter `http://aws.amazon.com/eclipse/` and hit *Enter*; this will display all the available plugins for AWS. You can either install everything or only the necessary components (it's better to install everything because there will be dependency between these plugins).

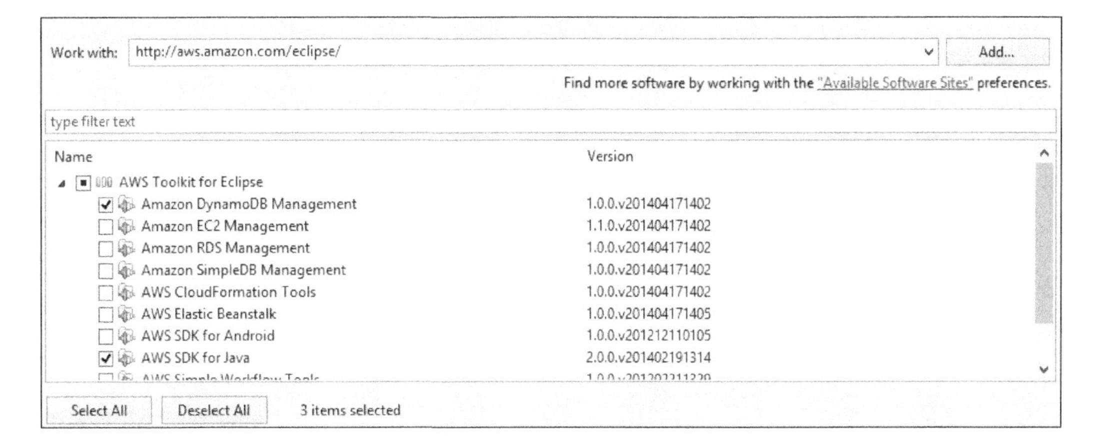

The following page will display the components that will be installed on Eclipse. Confirm them and proceed.

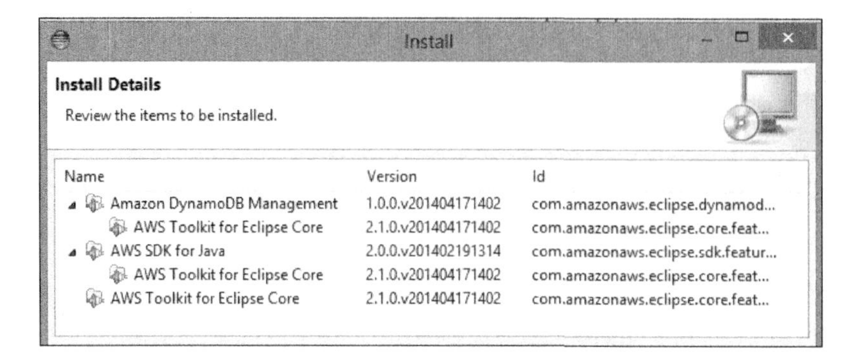

The following page will show the invalid components (**AWS SDK for Android** in the following screenshot). If the component not being installed does not cause any trouble, just proceed with the installation:

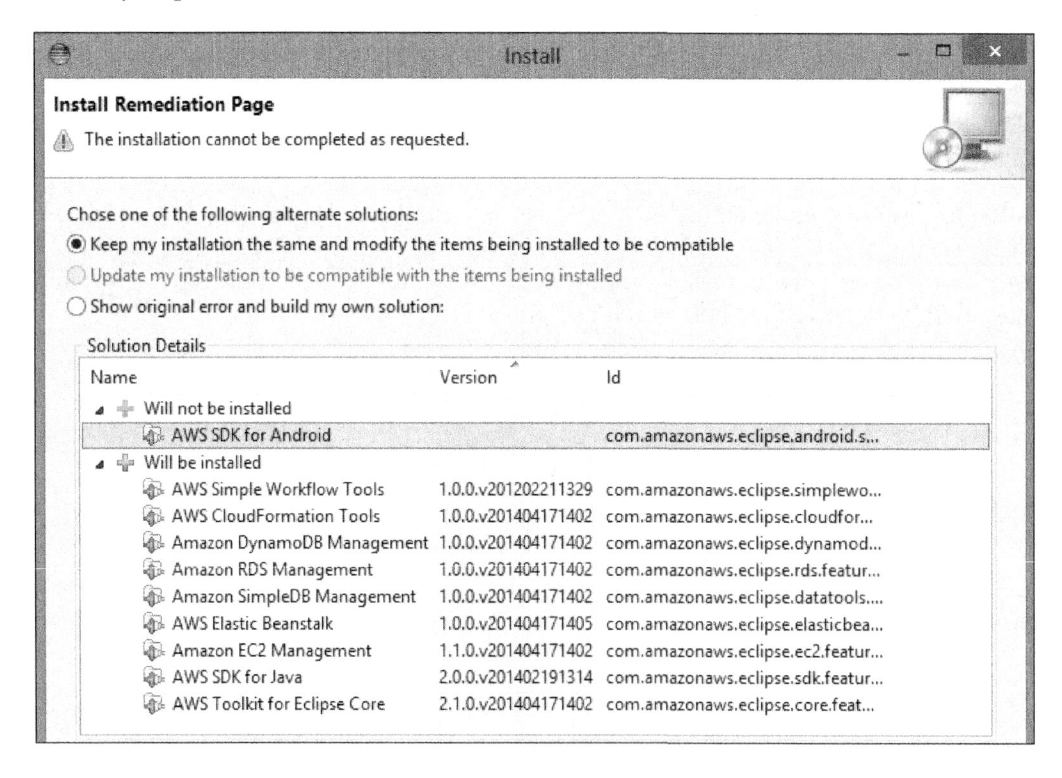

A security warning might be displayed; make sure you're installing from AWS and not from any third party. If you feel that the source is safe then proceed by clicking on **OK**.

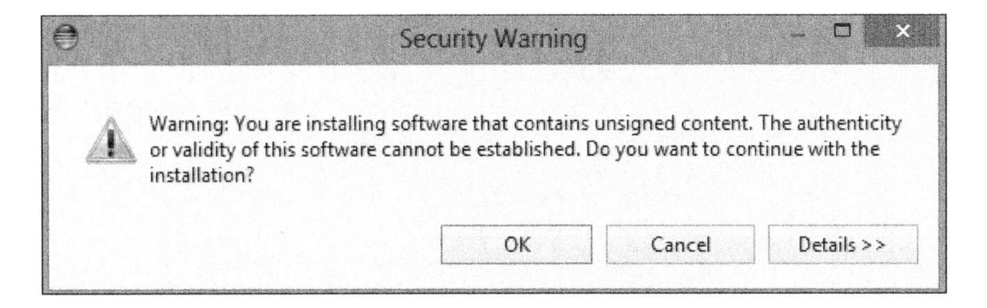

After successful installation, Eclipse will ask you to restart for the changes to take effect.

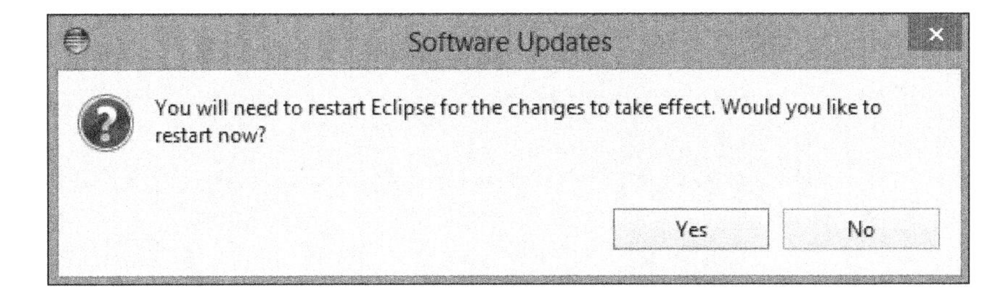

After restarting Eclipse, you can see a new AWS toolkit for Eclipse icon. The default Eclipse perspective will be Java. To open the perspective to work with DynamoDB, select **Window** | **Open Perspective**; it must show the first two perspectives as shown in the following screenshot. Double-click on **AWS Management** to begin our work.

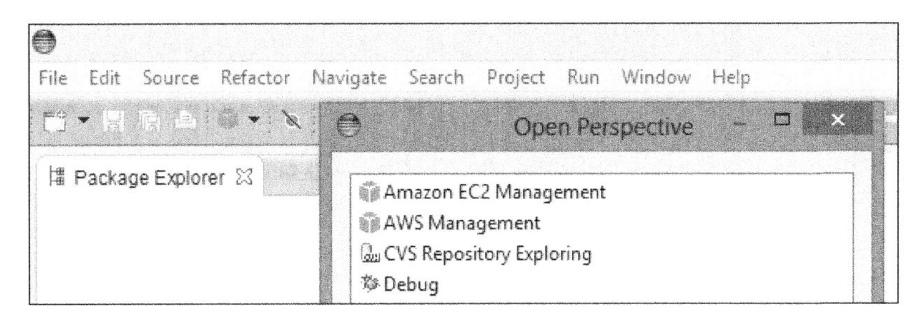

While working in the management console, we must login with our AWS username and password. However, in the case of the Eclipse plugin, we need to specify a few more attributes (such as **Access Key ID** and **Secret Access Key**, which can be obtained from the management console's **Security Credentials** page) for authentication. We can specify our account details by clicking on the AWS toolkit for Eclipse icon and selecting the **Preferences** option.

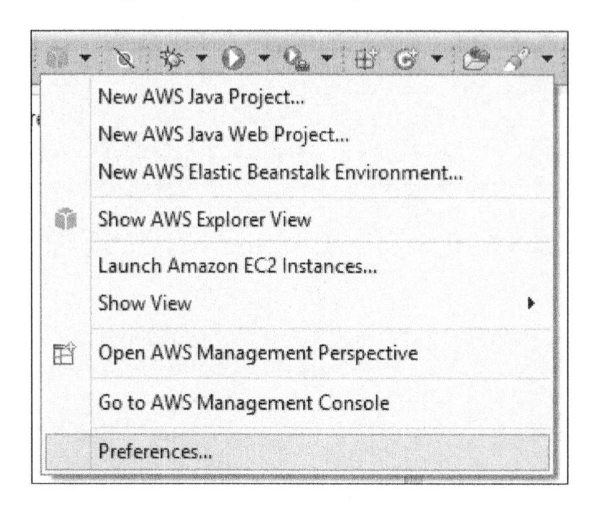

The following pop-up window will ask for details, which we can fetch from the security page in the management console:

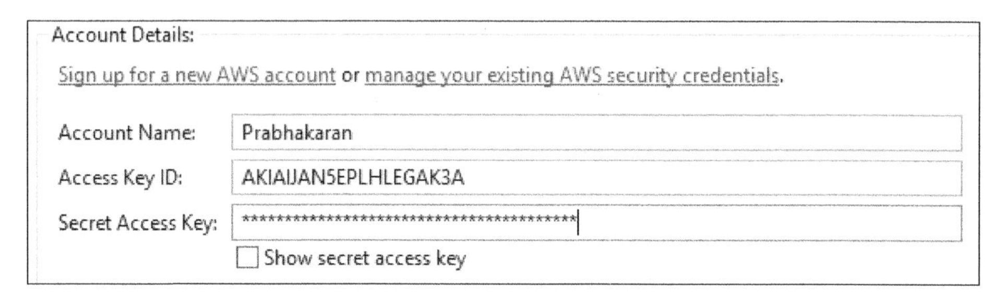

Once the configuration is successful, all the AWS components will be loaded. We can right-click on the corresponding service and refresh to get the latest data. The icon in the top-right corner with the US flag is the region we have currently selected. If the DynamoDB table was created in the eastern region of the USA using the management console and if we then select the US-west region here in Eclipse, you will never see that table in our perspective.

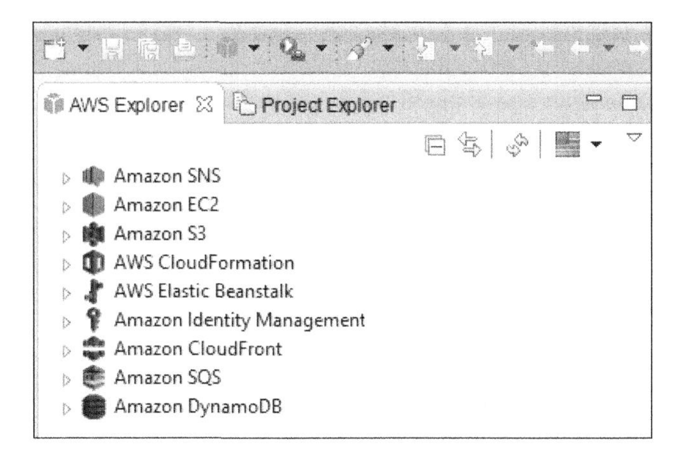

We can change the region by just clicking on the dropdown beside the flag in the top-right corner.

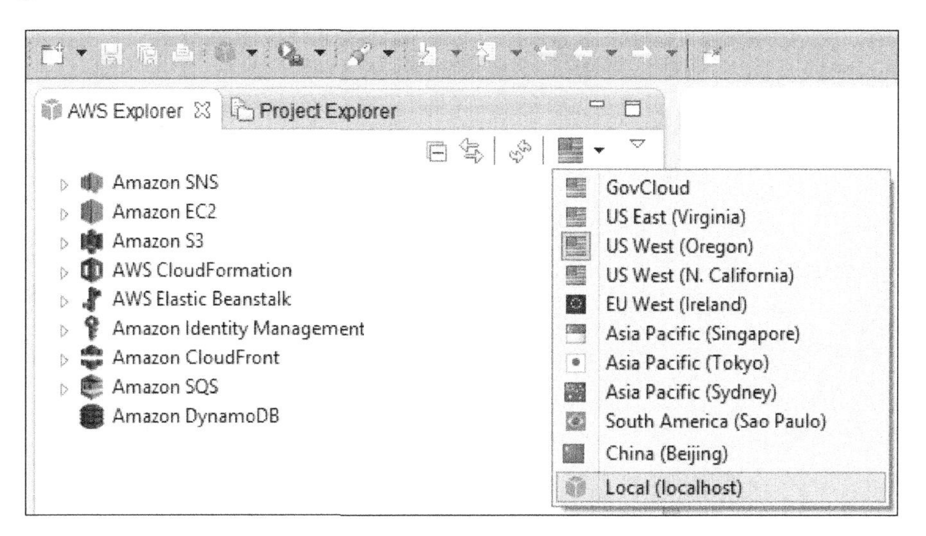

Once the desired region is selected, right-click on DynamoDB and choose the **Create Table** option.

The **Create Table** option will open the following page, asking us for the mandatory parameters to be passed while creating a table:

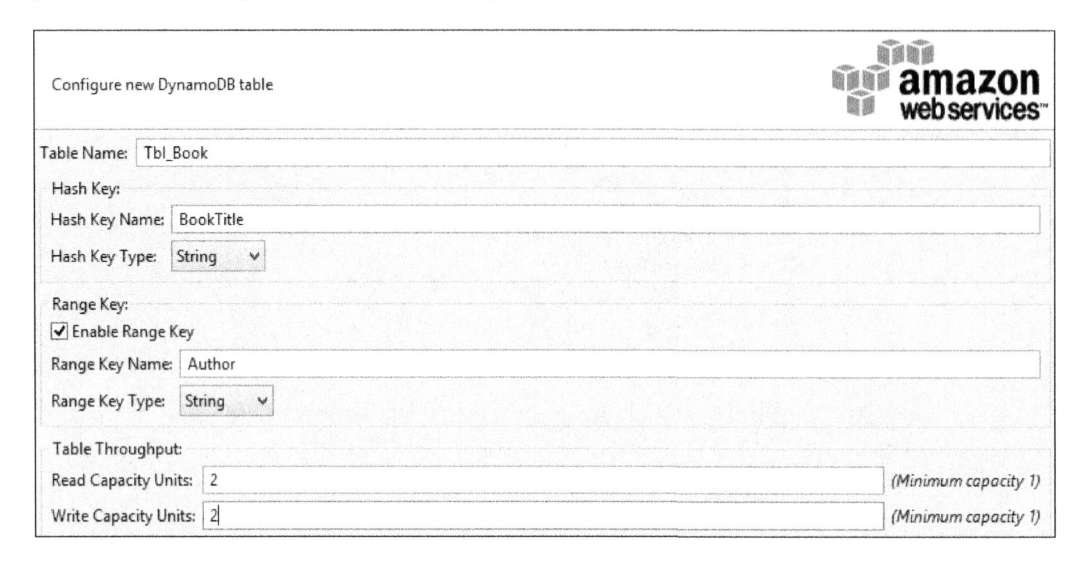

Since the index also has to be created along with the table, we need to specify the secondary indexes (if any) here:

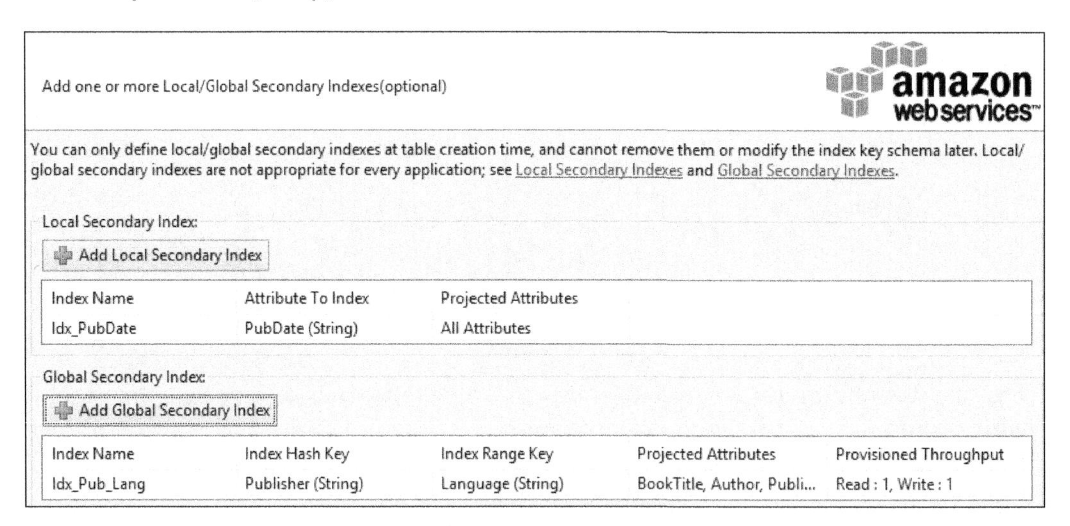

After that, the table will be created and it becomes active:

Double-clicking on the table name will open the following tab. In this tab, there will be five icons (just below the table name); we will look at the functionalities of each icon in the next page. Now we need to focus only on the last icon, which is used to add attributes to the table.

Clicking on the Add attribute column icon will open the following window, asking us to enter the name of the attribute to be created (it will not ask for the type).

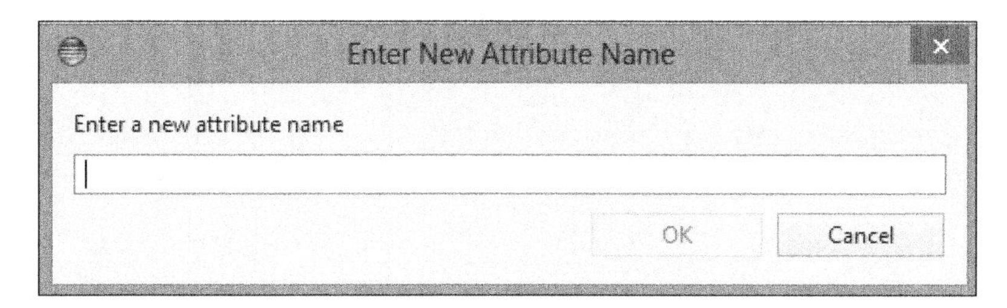

After adding the necessary attributes, click on the grid to insert the value. By default all attributes will be treated as `String`. To change it to the `Number` type, just click on the **a** button in the **Publisher** attribute, as shown in the following screenshot:

Clicking on the button a will open a dropdown from which we can choose whether we want the field to be `String` or `Number`. I hear your question: how can I insert the `Set` data type? The answer is shown in the next screenshot:

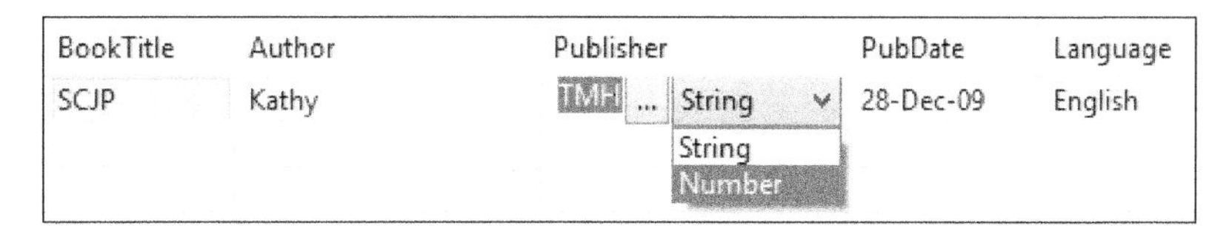

To change an attribute type from normal to `Set`, just click on the button with ellipses (**...**). This will open an **Edit values** window, asking whether we need to make this attribute `String` or `StringSet`. Click on **<new value>** to add a new value to this set.

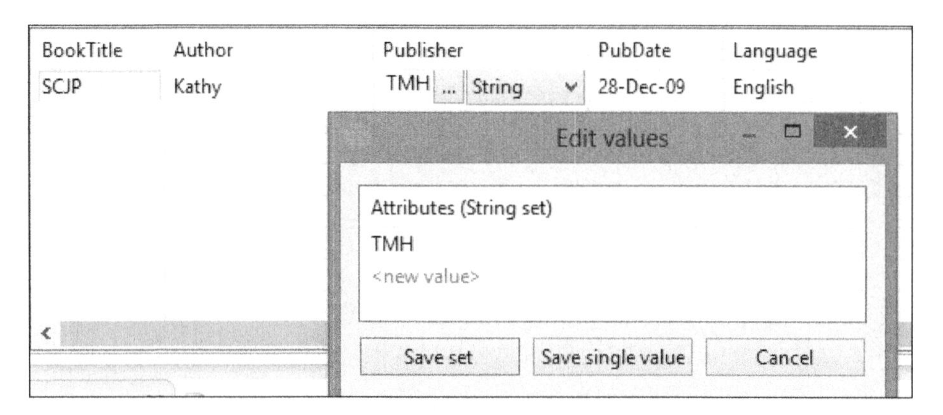

After inserting all the necessary attributes for an item, click on the grid below the item. The item with the attribute values entered will appear in red (which means the item is not saved into the table):

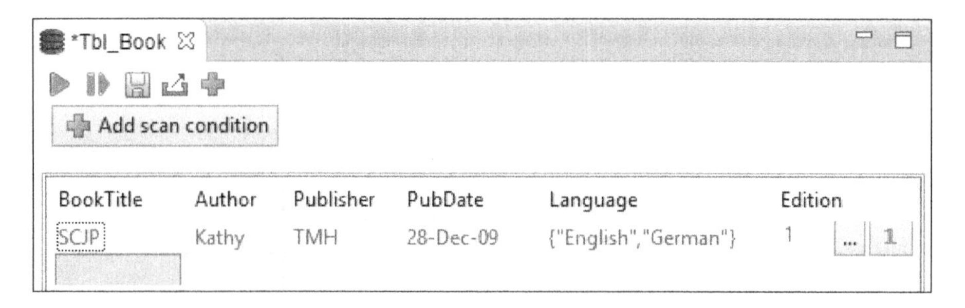

Now we can see the DynamoDB utility icons. The first icon is used to run a scan on the DynamoDB table, the second icon is used to pause the scan, the third is to save the items into the table, and the fourth icon is used to export table data into a CSV file. The last icon is used to add an attribute to the DynamoDB table.

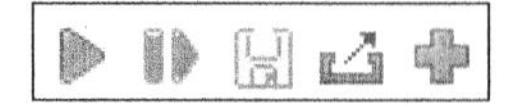

Let's see how to scan a table using the Eclipse plugin. Clicking on the **Add scan condition** button in the previous screenshot will open the following configuration options. In the textbox next to the **Attribute** checkbox, enter the attribute name to be queried, select the comparison operation to be performed, enter the selection criteria, and click on the Scan icon (the first one). This will retrieve the result.

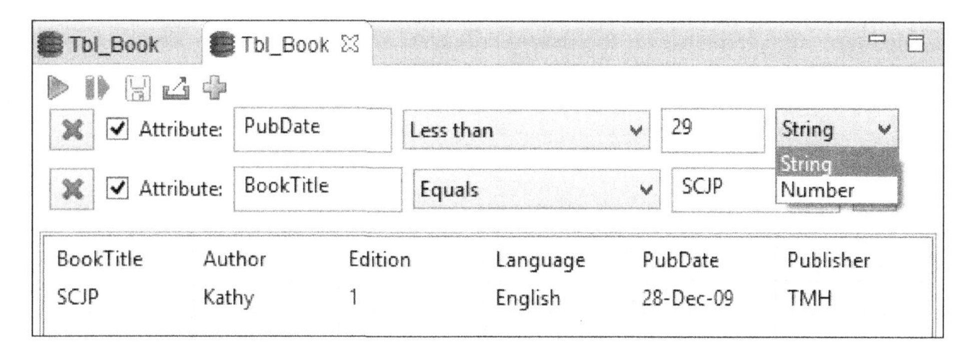

The command-line interface

You can't beat classics, can you? Even though the previous two interfaces provide easy usage of DynamoDB, the command-line interface provides good flexibility and it makes life simple for advanced programmers by reducing the number of clicks; instead of using the management console or the Eclipse plugin for DynamoDB interaction, we can write some commands and program it to do certain redundant jobs.

To get the AWS CLI, go to the link shown in the following screenshot:

Visit `https://s3.amazonaws.com/aws-cli/AWSCLI64.msi` to download the AWS CLI setup. Once the installation is complete, go to the path in the command prompt (the path might differ based on the platform, in my case the path is `C:\Program Files\Amazon\AWSCLI`). Run the `aws configure` command to configure CLI with our AWS credentials.

Hitting *Enter* will ask for the following four options:

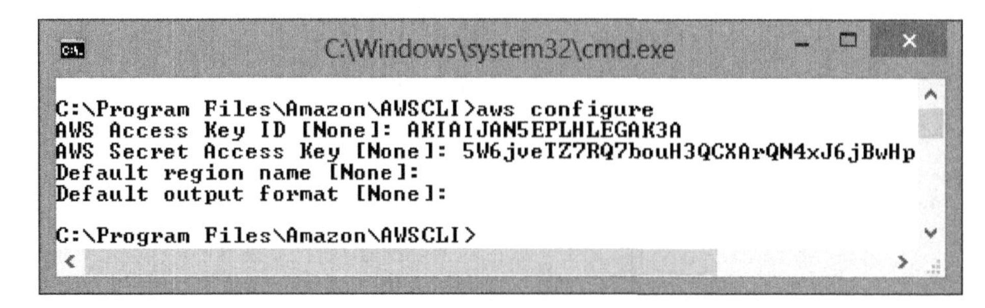

If we feel that any of the parameters have changed at all, type in `aws configure` again and provide the necessary details. It is also possible to leave certain parameters empty:

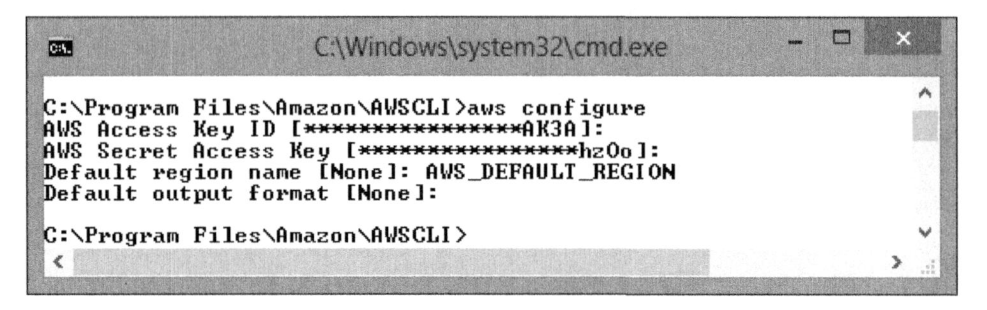

As shown in the following screenshot, running the `aws configure` command will replace the old parameters with the newer parameters:

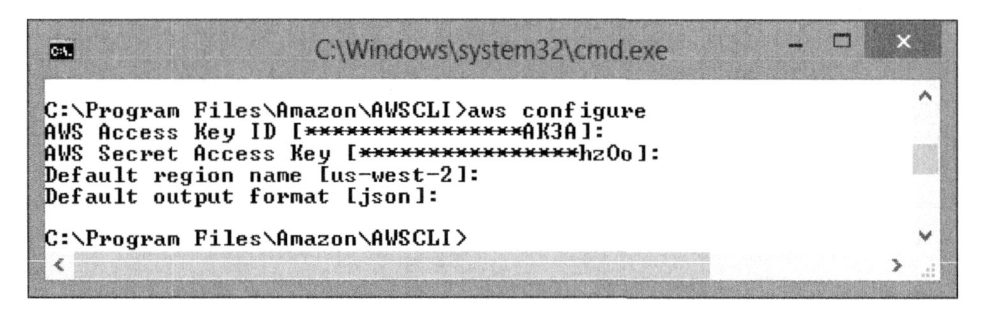

We will now see one of the simplest of the DynamoDB commands: table creation. We are going to create the same table we created using the management console (but without secondary indexes), with the help of the following command:

```
aws dynamodb create-table --table-name Tbl_Book

--attribute-definitions AttributeName=BookTitle,AttributeType=S
AttributeName=Author,AttributeType=S --key-schema
AttributeName=BookTitle,KeyType=HASH
AttributeName=Author,KeyType=RANGE

--provisioned-throughput ReadCapacityUnits=2,WriteCapacityUnits=2
```

Once you provide the command to create a table, you can find the JSON table that will give information about the table creation.

```
Command Prompt
Microsoft Windows [Version 6.2.9200]
(c) 2012 Microsoft Corporation. All rights reserved.

C:\Users\ADMIN>cd C:\Program Files\Amazon\AWSCLI

C:\Program Files\Amazon\AWSCLI>aws dynamodb create-table --table-name Tbl_Book -
-attribute-definitions AttributeName=BookTitle,AttributeType=S AttributeName=Aut
hor,AttributeType=S --key-schema AttributeName=BookTitle,KeyType=HASH AttributeN
ame=Author,KeyType=RANGE --provisioned-throughput ReadCapacityUnits=2,WriteCapac
ityUnits=2
```


```
{
    "TableDescription": {
        "AttributeDefinitions": [
            {
                "AttributeName": "Author",
                "AttributeType": "S"
            },
            {
                "AttributeName": "BookTitle",
                "AttributeType": "S"
            }
        ],
        "ProvisionedThroughput": {
            "NumberOfDecreasesToday": 0,
            "WriteCapacityUnits": 2,
            "ReadCapacityUnits": 2
        },
        "TableSizeBytes": 0,
        "TableName": "Tbl_Book",
        "TableStatus": "CREATING",
        "KeySchema": [
            {
                "KeyType": "HASH",
                "AttributeName": "BookTitle"
            },
            {
                "KeyType": "RANGE",
                "AttributeName": "Author"
            }
        ],
        "ItemCount": 0,
        "CreationDateTime": 1399866740.037
    }
}
```


The returned JSON will describe the table created.

In the following screenshot, we will be performing two operations. The first step is retrieving all the table names in the configured region using the `aws dynamodb list-tables` command. The second command `aws dynamodb describe-table --table-name Tbl_Book` is for describing a table:

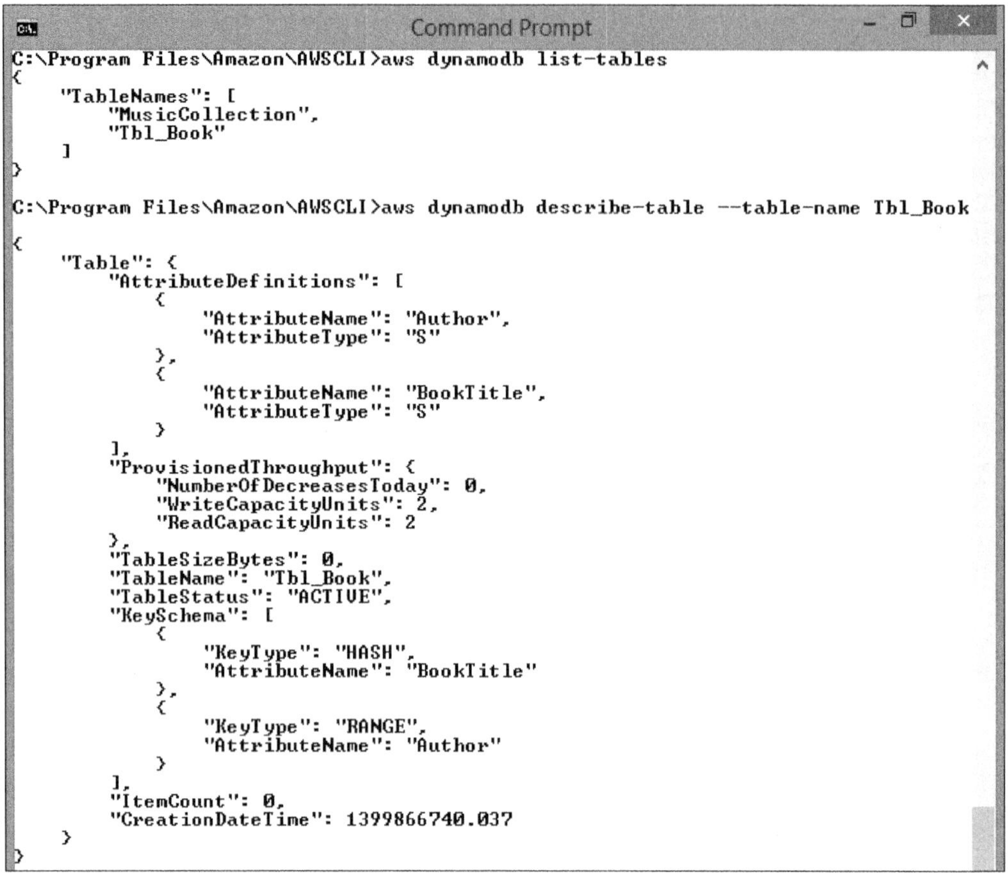

```
Command Prompt
C:\Program Files\Amazon\AWSCLI>aws dynamodb list-tables
{
    "TableNames": [
        "MusicCollection",
        "Tbl_Book"
    ]
}

C:\Program Files\Amazon\AWSCLI>aws dynamodb describe-table --table-name Tbl_Book

{
    "Table": {
        "AttributeDefinitions": [
            {
                "AttributeName": "Author",
                "AttributeType": "S"
            },
            {
                "AttributeName": "BookTitle",
                "AttributeType": "S"
            }
        ],
        "ProvisionedThroughput": {
            "NumberOfDecreasesToday": 0,
            "WriteCapacityUnits": 2,
            "ReadCapacityUnits": 2
        },
        "TableSizeBytes": 0,
        "TableName": "Tbl_Book",
        "TableStatus": "ACTIVE",
        "KeySchema": [
            {
                "KeyType": "HASH",
                "AttributeName": "BookTitle"
            },
            {
                "KeyType": "RANGE",
                "AttributeName": "Author"
            }
        ],
        "ItemCount": 0,
        "CreationDateTime": 1399866740.037
    }
}
```

The following screenshot shows how an item can be inserted into the DynamoDB table. This command purely depends on the OS in which AWS CLI is installed. For Windows 8 the command is as follows:

```
aws dynamodb put-item --table-name Tbl_Book --item
{\"BookTitle\":{\"S\":\"SCJP\"},\"Author\":{\"S\":\"Kathy\"},
\"Language\":{\"S\":\"English\"},\"Editions\":{\"NS\":[\"1\",\"2\"]}}
--return-consumed-capacity TOTAL
```

If the command throws an error for other platforms, we just need to replace `\"` with `"`, as shown in the following code:

```
aws dynamodb put-item --table-name Tbl_Book --item
{"BookTitle":{"S":"SCJP"},"Author":{"S":"Kathy"},
"Language":{"S":"English"},"Editions":{"NS":["1","2"]}}
--return-consumed-capacity TOTAL
```

Now it will work fine. Otherwise type `aws dynamodb put-item help` to retrieve the format in which the request has to be made.

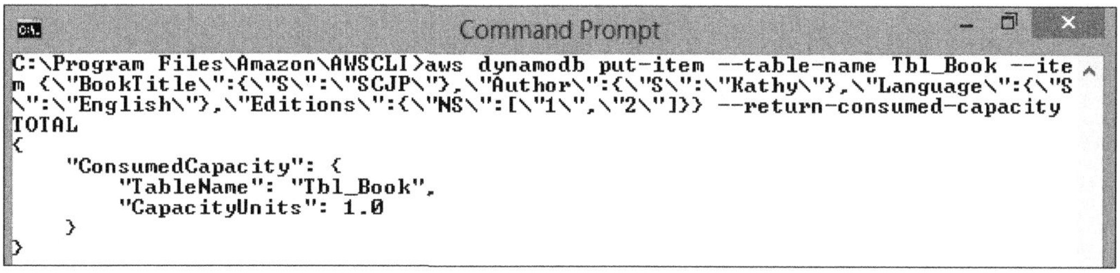

```
Command Prompt
C:\Program Files\Amazon\AWSCLI>aws dynamodb put-item --table-name Tbl_Book --ite
m {\"BookTitle\":{\"S\":\"SCJP\"},\"Author\":{\"S\":\"Kathy\"},\"Language\":{\"S
\":\"English\"},\"Editions\":{\"NS\":[\"1\",\"2\"]}} --return-consumed-capacity
TOTAL
{
    "ConsumedCapacity": {
        "TableName": "Tbl_Book",
        "CapacityUnits": 1.0
    }
}
```

The following command inserts two items into the table. While inserting a set, the set values must be enclosed in [] (square brackets) and each value must be delimited by `,` (comma). Let me write both the commands in a textbox to make it easier to understand:

```
aws dynamodb put-item --table-name Tbl_Book --item
{\"BookTitle\":{\"S\":\"SCJP\"},\"Author\":{\"S\":\"Simon\"},
\"Language\":{\"S\":\"English\"},\"Editions\":{\"NS\":[\"3\",\"6\"]}}
--return-consumed-capacity TOTAL
```

The following `put-item` command will insert an item with the new `Type` attribute:

```
aws dynamodb put-item --table-name Tbl_Book --item
{\"BookTitle\":{\"S\":\"Inferno\"},\"Author\":{\"S\":\"DanBrown\"},
\"Language\":{\"S\":\"English\"},\"Editions\":{\"NS\":[\"1\"]},
\"Type\":{\"S\":\"Fiction\"}}
--return-consumed-capacity TOTAL
```

After writing successful syntax of the command, you can see the JSON format of the table data and the item will be added to it.

```
Command Prompt
C:\Program Files\Amazon\AWSCLI>aws dynamodb put-item --table-name Tbl_Book --ite
m {\"BookTitle\":{\"S\":\"SCJP\"},\"Author\":{\"S\":\"Simon\"},\"Language\":{\"S
\":\"English\"},\"Editions\":{\"NS\":[\"3\",\"6\"]}} --return-consumed-capacity
TOTAL
{
    "ConsumedCapacity": {
        "TableName": "Tbl_Book",
        "CapacityUnits": 1.0
    }
}

C:\Program Files\Amazon\AWSCLI>aws dynamodb put-item --table-name Tbl_Book --ite
m {\"BookTitle\":{\"S\":\"Inferno\"},\"Author\":{\"S\":\"DanBrown\"},\"Language\
":{\"S\":\"English\"},\"Editions\":{\"NS\":[\"1\"]},\"Type\":{\"S\":\"Fiction\"}
 --return-consumed-capacity TOTAL

Error parsing parameter '--item': Invalid JSON: Expecting object: line 1 column
128 (char 127)
JSON received: {"BookTitle":{"S":"Inferno"},"Author":{"S":"DanBrown"},"Language"
:{"S":"English"},"Editions":{"NS":["1"]},"Type":{"S":"Fiction"}

C:\Program Files\Amazon\AWSCLI>aws dynamodb put-item --table-name Tbl_Book --ite
m {\"BookTitle\":{\"S\":\"Inferno\"},\"Author\":{\"S\":\"DanBrown\"},\"Language\
":{\"S\":\"English\"},\"Editions\":{\"NS\":[\"1\"]},\"Type\":{\"S\":\"Fiction\"}
} --return-consumed-capacity TOTAL
{
    "ConsumedCapacity": {
        "TableName": "Tbl_Book",
        "CapacityUnits": 1.0
    }
}
```

The command written in between the other two valid commands for `put-item` is not valid as it gives me an error. Can you guess why? It's because I missed closing the `--item` JSON (I missed out } before `--return-consumed-capacity`).

> Capacity unit is the measure of data size written into (or read from) DynamoDB. It is rounded off to the next 1 KB size. What this means is, if we try to write 1.01 KB of data, DynamoDB consumes 2 capacity units. Even while writing 1.99 KB (or even 2 KB) of data, DynamoDB consumes 2 capacity units. Whenever we insert an item using the `put-item` command (even if the item size is 0.2 KB), it will consume 1 capacity unit at least.

The following screenshot tries to scan a DynamoDB table. The command used to scan a table with name `Tbl_Book` is `aws dynamodb scan --table-name Tbl_Book`:

```
Command Prompt
C:\Program Files\Amazon\AWSCLI>aws dynamodb scan --table-name Tbl_Book
{
    "Items": [
        {
            "Editions": {
                "NS": [
                    "2",
                    "1"
                ]
            },
            "BookTitle": {
                "S": "SCJP"
            },
            "Language": {
                "S": "English"
            },
            "Author": {
                "S": "Kathy"
            }
        },
        {
            "Editions": {
                "NS": [
                    "3",
                    "6"
                ]
            },
            "BookTitle": {
                "S": "SCJP"
            },
            "Language": {
                "S": "English"
            },
            "Author": {
                "S": "Simon"
            }
        },
        {
            "Editions": {
                "NS": [
                    "1"
                ]
            },
            "BookTitle": {
                "S": "Inferno"
            },
            "Type": {
                "S": "Fiction"
            },
            "Language": {
                "S": "English"
            },
            "Author": {
                "S": "DanBrown"
            }
        }
    ]
```

There are several other commands available in AWS CLI that are not listed in this chapter. We can get those commands and their working syntax using the `aws dynamodb help` command.

```
Aws dynamodb --help
```

This will list the following options:

- `batch-get-item`
- `batch-write-item`
- `delete-item`
- `delete-table`
- `describe-table`
- `get-item`
- `help`
- `query`
- `update-item`
- `update-table`

Some options that we have already discussed are not listed here, such as `create-table`, `list-tables`, `put-item`, and `scan`.

Summary

In this chapter we gained an insight into accessing DynamoDB in the management console and command line. We also took a look at the Eclipse plugin.

The chapter started with the DynamoDB table and item operations using the management console and we saw how to create a table with the necessary primary key and secondary index. Then we also discussed how to work on a table item. After that we configured our Eclipse IDE with the AWS plugin, created a table with secondary indexes, and then inserted a few items into the table. We then discussed how to make use of the table's primary key attributes and secondary index key attributes while querying that DynamoDB table. We also discussed how to change the region (or location) in which DynamoDB has to perform its operation. We saw how to download the AWS command-line tool and its configuration setup in our local system. Then we executed a few commands through the command-line interface, which performed the same DynamoDB operations as performed in the previous two interfaces.

The management console, the Eclipse IDE with AWS plugin, and the command-line interface cannot go beyond a certain limit. For example, even to test (syntax and usage) an application locally (syntax and usage), we need to connect to AWS every time. So you might ask me whether it is possible to emulate AWS DynamoDB in my local PC. The answer is yes! This is what we are going to discuss next.

In the next chapter, we will learn about DynamoDB locals and CLI commands. We will also learn to use CLI from a developer's or DBA's perspective.

3

Tools and Libraries of AWS DynamoDB

We have understood the strength of the Eclipse plugin in the previous chapter on interfaces. We have seen a few of the basic operations using three interfaces. But along with those interfaces, DynamoDB supports lots of tools and libraries. In this chapter, we will see one such tool that is used along with the Eclipse IDE. We will mostly perform DynamoDB operations using the Java SDK. In this chapter, we will cover the following topics:

- Creating an SDK project
- SDK operations
- DynamoDB Local

We can easily create tables, indexes, attributes, and items. After doing all of these offline, we can commit or save to AWS DynamoDB. This is the use of DynamoDB Local.

If we need to insert event data (which is available as a CSV file) into DynamoDB, are we comfortable looking at the CSV file manually and creating one item for every event and finally put it into the table? Is it possible to perform the operation if the item size of the CSV file goes beyond a million records? Obviously the answer is no, because it requires a lot of patience and some errors might occur as we are all human and *to err is human*.

Another possible case is that we have developed a web application (let's say, a JSF application) for the library catalogue, which we have discussed in *Chapter 2, DynamoDB Interfaces*, and we have decided to use DynamoDB as the database. Now the biggest challenge would be integrating DynamoDB with Java. This is where the SDK comes into the picture. By importing and including certain DynamoDB libraries, we can play with DynamoDB using simple Java code.

Along with Java, DynamoDB supports SDK for PHP and .NET too. Some limited support is available for JavaScript, Python, Android, iOS, and Ruby too. Since Java is the one that is easy to learn, and is open source as well, we will discuss Java AWS SDK in this chapter.

If you're able to recall, before performing a DynamoDB operation using either the Eclipse plugin or AWS CLI, we authenticated ourselves to AWS using our credentials. We need to do the same here as well. So in order to proceed further we must configure our Eclipse to access DynamoDB. Refer to the *The Eclipse plugin* section in *Chapter 2, DynamoDB Interfaces*.

Once we have added our AWS account details to Eclipse, it automatically adds these properties to a file named AwsCredentials.properties. This file will be located at $USER_HOME/.aws/config (in the case of Windows, its C://Users/<user-name>/.aws/config). If the file is not created then we can create it ourselves. The file will look as follows (a few characters are removed and replaced for security purposes):

```
[default]
aws_access_key_id = AKIAIJAN5EPLHLEGAK3A
aws_secret_access_key = 5W6jveT***Prabhakaran****xJ6jBwHpzM+hzOo
region = us-east-1
output = json
```

The first two lines (treating [default] as line zero) are to authenticate ourselves to AWS. If the file has credentials other than yours, then replace those and save it. The third line specifies the region in which we need to perform DynamoDB operations. The last line is to specify the output format (of the response from AWS).

Creating your first SDK project

If we have already installed the Eclipse plugin and are able to see the credentials file created correctly, then we are ready to fly on the SDK plane. Here's how:

1. Clicking on the AWS toolkit for the Eclipse icon will provide us with the option to create a new AWS project as shown:

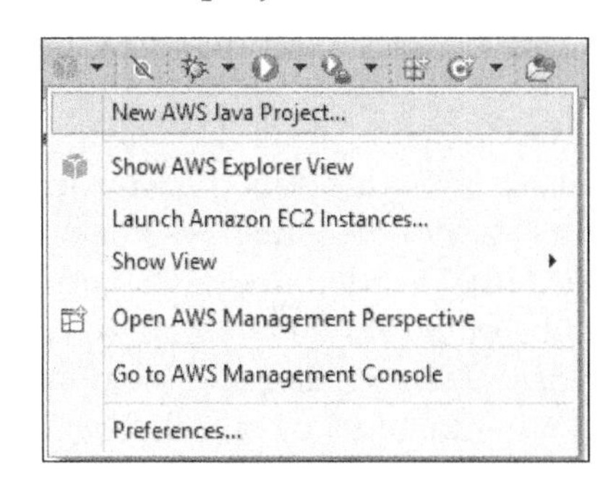

2. Here we need to select **New AWS Java Project....** Clicking on this option will open the following window. Clicking on this option for the first time will bring up a few sample codes from AWS and will ask whether we want these sample codes to be part of the project.
3. It is recommended that you check the **Amazon DynamoDB Sample** checkbox the first time, to understand the syntax of DynamoDB table operations.
4. Once done, select the AWS account that is already configured, or configure a new AWS account.
5. Click on the **Next** button to proceed.

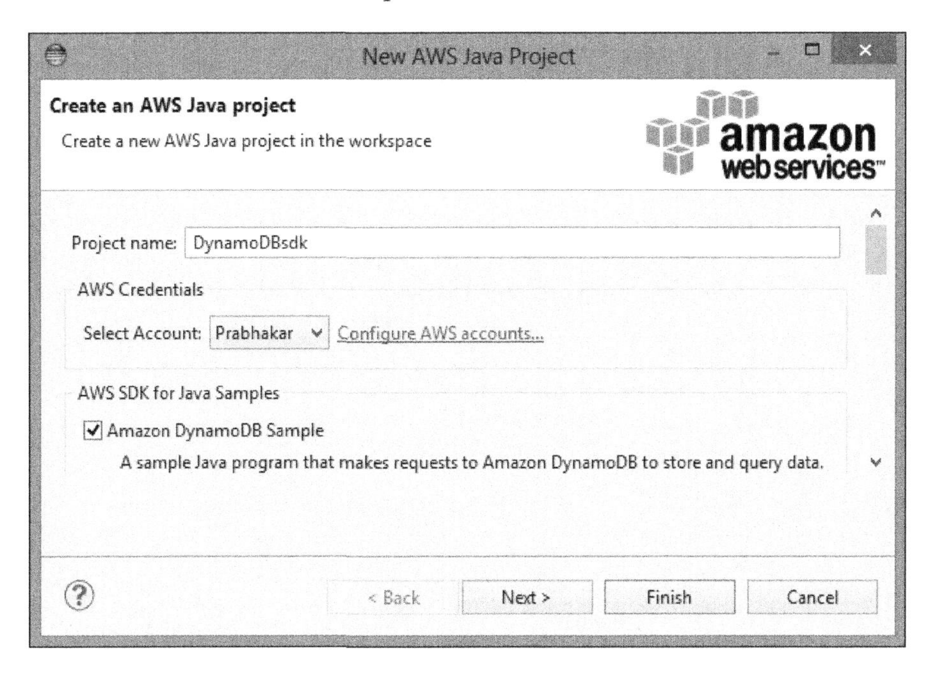

6. Clicking on the **Next** button will create a new project with the name specified in the previous window. The project structure is shown in the next screenshot.

7. The credentials file will be made available by default in the `src` folder of the project. The sample DynamoDB code will also be available in the default package of this `src` folder in a file named `AmazonDynamoDBSample.java`.

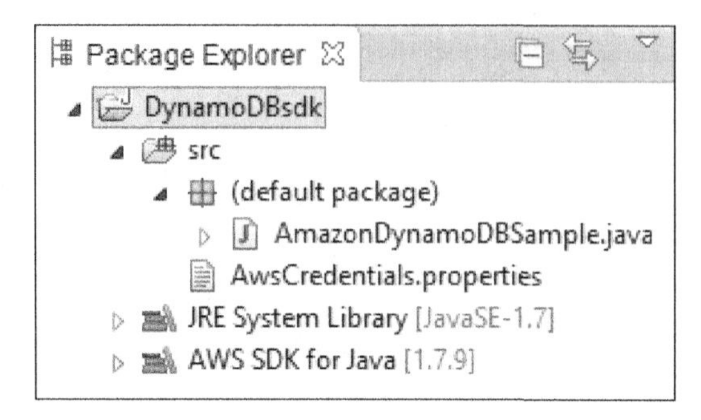

8. We can take a look at our credentials file by double-clicking on the `AwsCredentials.properties` file. The file content is as shown in the following screenshot (I have removed my complete secret key for security purposes. You are not supposed to share your keys with anyone; it is like leaving the safe door open. Anyone with your key can pretend to be you):

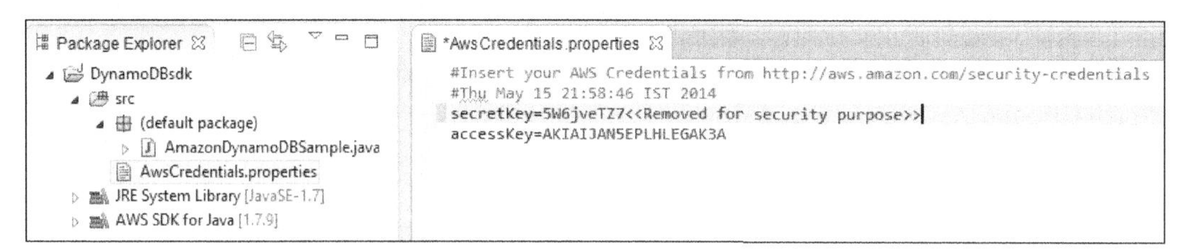

Even though the properties file is located in the project, while running any program through Eclipse it will always fetch the configuration information located at `$USER_HOME/.aws/config`. But it is not safe to place this credentials file at this location; AWS always wants us to keep this information at `$USER_HOME/.aws/credentials` (take a look at line 2 of the next screenshot).

Even if we provide invalid credential information in the project's properties file, while running the project the Eclipse IDE will fetch the correct credential information from the default location. Running the sample code will yield us the following output:

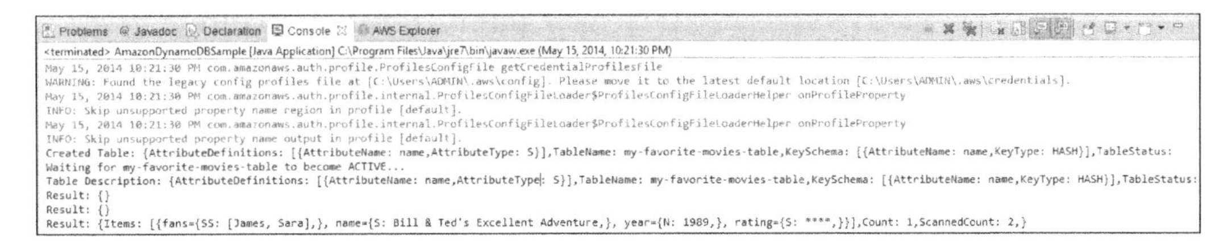

The first six lines in the previous screenshot are logger messages (warning, information, or error) and the remaining lines are the output syso (short way of calling `System.out.println`) print statements mentioned in the sample code.

I have deliberately modified the access key of the credentials file located at `$USER_HOME/.aws/config`. After that, if we try running the sample code it will throw the error `UnrecognizedClientException`.

This exception will be thrown only if the project is not able to instantiate the DynamoDB client, which is a clear indication that there is something wrong with the credentials. Take a look at the following screenshot:

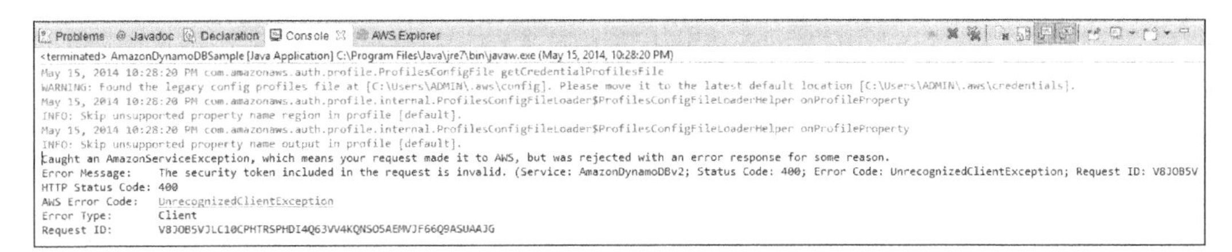

Since the sample code is provided by AWS itself, I don't want to get into trouble by providing the code here. So we will see what that sample code does. First and foremost, it creates a table named `my-favorite-movies-table` in the `US_WEST_2` region. Once we have run this code, we need to open AWS Explorer and refresh Amazon DynamoDB as follows:

Make sure that you've selected the correct region (`US_WEST_2`) in AWS Explorer; otherwise we cannot see the table getting created.

Double-clicking on the table name will open the following window showing the contents of the table:

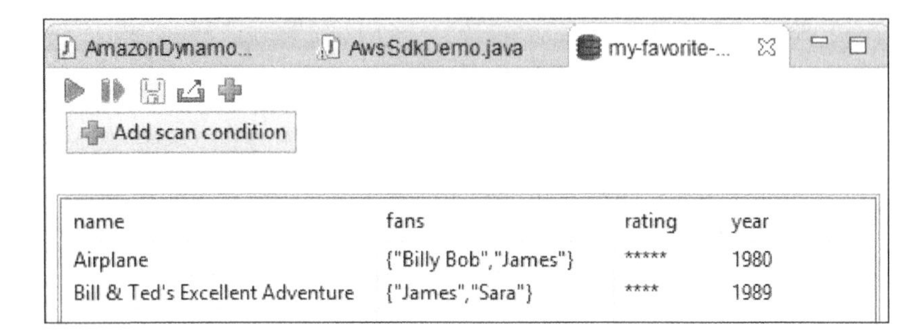

I hope that there is nothing I need to explain about the table's attribute names and types. In this table, `name` is the only key attribute.

The sample code (provided by Amazon SDK) will not have code to create any indexes. In the following sections we will discuss everything in detail. First we will create a new class named `AwsSdkDemo` in the same project.

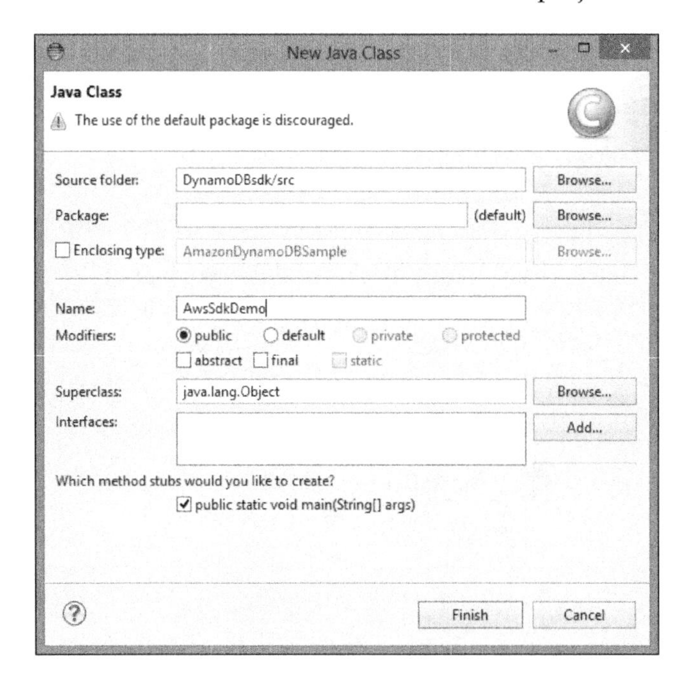

In this DynamoDB class (named `AwsSdkDemo`) we are going to perform the following DynamoDB operations:

- Initializing our AWS credentials
- Defining table attributes
- Defining the key schema (of table and indexes)
- Creating local and global secondary indexes
- Defining the provisioned throughput
- Creating a table with the parameters mentioned earlier
- Describing a table
- Updating the DynamoDB table
- Checking table status
- Adding (inserting) items to the table

Java SDK operations

There are eight user-defined private functions that are being invoked in the following code. We will see each and every function in detail:

```
public class AwsSdkDemo {

  static AmazonDynamoDBClient client;
  public static void main(String[] args) {
    try {

      initializeCredentials();
      String tableName = "Tbl_Book";

      if (Tables.doesTableExist(client, tableName)) {
        System.out.println("Table " + tableName + " already
          EXISTS");
      }
      else {
        ArrayList<AttributeDefinition> attributeDefinitions =
          getTableAttributes();
        ArrayList<KeySchemaElement> keySchemaElements =
          getTableKeySchema();
        LocalSecondaryIndex localSecondaryIndex =
          getLocalSecondaryIndex();
        ArrayList<LocalSecondaryIndex> localSecondaryIndexes =
          newArrayList<LocalSecondaryIndex>();
```

```
            localSecondaryIndexes.add(localSecondaryIndex);
            GlobalSecondaryIndex globalSecondaryIndex =
              getGlobalSecondaryIndex();
            ProvisionedThroughput provisionedThroughput =
              getProvisionedThroughput();

            CreateTableRequest request = new CreateTableRequest()
              .withTableName(tableName)
              .withAttributeDefinitions(attributeDefinitions)
              .withKeySchema(keySchemaElements)
              .withProvisionedThroughput(provisionedThroughput)
              .withGlobalSecondaryIndexes(globalSecondaryIndex);
            request.setLocalSecondaryIndexes(localSecondaryIndexes);

            CreateTableResult result = client.createTable(request);

            System.out.println("Waiting for " + tableName + " to
              become ACTIVE...");

            Tables.waitForTableToBecomeActive(client, tableName);
            TableDescription tableDescription = client.describeTable(
              new DescribeTableRequest()
            .withTableName(tableName))
            .getTable();

            System.out.println("Created Table: " + tableDescription);

            UpdateTableRequest updateTableRequest =
              getUpdateTableRequest(tableName);
            UpdateTableResult updateTableResult =
              client.updateTable(updateTableRequest);
            putItems(tableName);
        }}
        catch (Exception e) {
          e.printStackTrace();
        }
    }}
```

The first method `initializeCredentials` is to load our AWS credentials and authenticate ourselves to AWS to run the program, in order to perform DynamoDB operations.

For all kinds of DynamoDB operations that we wish to perform, we must do it through this client.

```
static AmazonDynamoDBClient client;
```

The following block will initialize the table name to the local variable. Then the `if` condition will check whether the table already exists with this name (on the client configured region) and return the Boolean value. If the table already exists then the syso message will be printed.

```
String tableName = "Tbl_Book";
if (Tables.doesTableExist(client, tableName)) {
  System.out.println("Table " + tableName + " already EXISTS");
}
```

The following block will create `CreateTableRequest` with attributes such as table name, attribute definitions, key schema, provisioned throughput, and indexes:

```
CreateTableRequest request = new CreateTableRequest()
  .withTableName(tableName)
  .withAttributeDefinitions(attributeDefinitions)
  .withKeySchema(keySchemaElements)
  .withProvisionedThroughput(provisionedThroughput)
  .withGlobalSecondaryIndexes(globalSecondaryIndex);
```

The following line will submit the table creation request through the DynamoDB client:

```
client.createTable(request);
```

The following line of code will pause the further execution of the code until the table becomes active (most probably used before adding items to the table):

```
Tables.waitForTableToBecomeActive(client, tableName);
```

The following code will request to describe the table name passed as a parameter to the client:

```
client.describeTable(new DescribeTableRequest()
  .withTableName(tableName))
  .getTable();
```

The following code will update a table with the passed `UpdateTableRequest` instance:

```
client.updateTable(updateTableRequest);
```

The default location of the credential file is `$USER_HOME/.aws/credentials`. But we have to keep our credentials file at `$USER_HOME/.aws/config` so that the SDK easily identifies them. In the following code:

- The first line of the `try` block will load the default AWS credentials
- The second line will configure the DynamoDB client with the loaded credential
- The third line will initialize the region to `US_WEST_2`, which is Oregon
- The last line of the `try` block will set the region for the DynamoDB client to `US-WEST-2`

In the event of the improper location of the credentials file, an exception will be thrown as follows:

```
private static void initializeCredentials() throws Exception {
  AWSCredentials credentials = null;
  try {
    credentials = new ProfileCredentialsProvider().getCredentials();
    client = new AmazonDynamoDBClient(credentials);
    Region usWest2 = Region.getRegion(Regions.US_WEST_2);
    client.setRegion(usWest2);
  } catch (Exception e) {
    throw new AmazonClientException(
    "Invalid location or format of credentials file.",e);
  }
}
```

The following function will prepare an `ArrayList`, which adds all the `AttributeDefinition` instances to it. Each `AttributeDefinition` will take two parameters: the first is the attribute name and the second is its attribute type, as shown in the following code. In the following code, we are defining five attributes:

```
private static ArrayList<AttributeDefinition>
  getTableAttributes() {
  ArrayList<AttributeDefinition> attributeDefinitions =
    newArrayList<AttributeDefinition>();
  attributeDefinitions.add(new AttributeDefinition()
    .withAttributeName("BookTitle")
    .withAttributeType("S"));
  attributeDefinitions.add(new AttributeDefinition()
    .withAttributeName("Author")
    .withAttributeType("S"));
  attributeDefinitions.add(new AttributeDefinition()
    .withAttributeName("PubDate")
    .withAttributeType("S"));
```

```
    attributeDefinitions.add(new AttributeDefinition()
      .withAttributeName("Publisher")
      .withAttributeType("S"));
    attributeDefinitions.add(new AttributeDefinition()
      .withAttributeName("Edition")
      .withAttributeType("N"));
    return attributeDefinitions;
  }
```

The next method will return `ArrayList` of the `KeySchemaElement` type. To this `ArrayList`, we are adding two `KeySchemaElement`. The first element is to set the `BookTitle` attribute as the hash key type and the second element is to set the `Author` attribute as the range key type. Finally we return this `ArrayList` as shown in the following code:

```
  private static ArrayList<KeySchemaElement> getTableKeySchema() {
    ArrayList<KeySchemaElement> ks =
      newArrayList<KeySchemaElement>();
    ks.add(new KeySchemaElement()
      .withAttributeName("BookTitle")
      .withKeyType(KeyType.HASH));
    ks.add(new KeySchemaElement()
      .withAttributeName("Author")
      .withKeyType(KeyType.RANGE));
    return ks;
  }
```

The next method will return a `ProvisionedThroughput` instance with the populated read/write throughput capacities for our table. The long number (`2L`) here means the maximum read or write data size per second. This is usually measured in kB/s. So here we are restricting the read/write speed to 2 kB/s. Have a look at the following code:

```
  private static ProvisionedThroughput getProvisionedThroughput() {
    ProvisionedThroughput provisionedThroughput =
      newProvisionedThroughput()
        .withReadCapacityUnits(2L)
        .withWriteCapacityUnits(2L);
    return provisionedThroughput;
  }
```

The following code tries to update the already created table; here we are modifying only the `ProvisionedThroughput` capacity units. During table creation we have set this value to `2L`; now we are updating it to `4L`. The `UpdateTableRequest` instance will allow us to change only a few parameters such as changing the provisioned throughput capacity of the table and (if required) the secondary index throughput capacity. If you have the question, say can we update (add or remove) secondary indexes of the table? The answer is no: we cannot add or remove secondary indexes using `UpdateTableRequest`.

We can specify an index for a table only during table creation. After that, we cannot update or add a secondary index.

```
private static UpdateTableRequest getUpdateTableRequest
  (String tableName) {
  ProvisionedThroughput upt = new ProvisionedThroughput()
    .withReadCapacityUnits(4L)
    .withWriteCapacityUnits(4L);

  UpdateTableRequest updateTableRequest = newUpdateTableRequest()
    .withTableName(tableName)
    .withProvisionedThroughput(upt);
  return updateTableRequest;
}
```

In the following function, we will try to put two items (`item1` and `item2`, each of type `Map<String, AttributeValue>`) into the table (whose name is taken as an input parameter). As we discussed earlier (the `getTableKeySchema` method), every item must have primary key attributes (`BookTitle` and `Author` attributes). So both the items have these two attributes.

In the first item (`item1`), including primary key attributes, we are adding four more attributes, namely `Publisher` (`String` type), `PubDate` (`String` type), `Language` (`StringSet` type), and `Edition` (`Number` type). In order to add the attributes we must call the correct method of the `AttributeValue` class, depending on the type of attribute we need to put.

In the second item (`item2`), we also add the same attributes for another book, with the additional attribute named `Pages` (`Number` type).

```
private static void putItems(String tableName) {
  Map<String, AttributeValue> item1 = new HashMap<String,
    AttributeValue>();
  item1.put("BookTitle", new AttributeValue().withS("SCJP"));
  item1.put("Author", new AttributeValue().withS("Kathy"));
```

```
    item1.put("Publisher", new AttributeValue().withS("TMH"));
    item1.put("PubDate", new AttributeValue().withS("28-Dec-09"));
    item1.put("Language", new AttributeValue()
      .withSS(Arrays.asList("English", "German")));
    item1.put("Edition", new AttributeValue().withN("1"));
    PutItemRequest putItemRequest = new PutItemRequest()
      .withTableName(tableName)
      .withItem(item1);
    client.putItem(putItemRequest);

    Map<String, AttributeValue> item2 = new HashMap<String,
      AttributeValue>();
    item2.put("BookTitle", new AttributeValue().withS("Inferno"));
    item2.put("Author", new AttributeValue().withS("DanBrown"));
    item2.put("Publisher", new AttributeValue().withS("TMH"));
    item2.put("PubDate", new AttributeValue().withS("28-Jul-12"));
    item2.put("Language", new AttributeValue()
      .withSS(Arrays.asList("English")));
    item2.put("Edition", new AttributeValue().withN("1"));
    item2.put("Pages", new AttributeValue().withN("623"));
    PutItemRequest putItemRequest1 = new PutItemRequest()
      .withTableName(tableName)
      .withItem(item2);
    client.putItem(putItemRequest1);
  }
```

In the `getTableAttributes` method, we have not specified or defined the `Pages` and `Language` attributes.

While creating the table, we must specify the primary key and index attributes; all other optional attributes can be specified during item insertion. The `Pages` and `Language` attributes, being non-key and non-index attributes, are not part of `AttributeDefinition` in the `getTableAttributes` method.

There are two more local functions invoked to create indexes, which we will see in the next chapter.

DynamoDB Local

DynamoDB Local is a local client-side database that emulates the DynamoDB database in our local system. This is pretty helpful while developing an application that uses DynamoDB as the backend. Every time after writing a module, in order to test whether the code works fine, we need to connect to Amazon and run it. This will consume a lot of bandwidth and a few dollars. To avoid this we can make use of DynamoDB Local and test the code locally. Once the testing is done we can then make our application use the AWS DynamoDB service. You need to perform only three actions for this, which are as follows:

1. Download DynamoDB Local from `http://dynamodb-local.s3-website-us-west-2.amazonaws.com/dynamodb_local_latest`.
2. Start the DynamoDB Local service (should have JRE 6 or later).
3. Point the code to use the DynamoDB Local port.

We don't need to discuss more about how to download a file from the Internet. So, let's go directly to step 2. The downloaded file might be a zipped one (`tar.gz` or `zip` or `rar`). We need to extract it to a location. I have extracted it to `C:\dynamodb` as shown in the following screenshot:

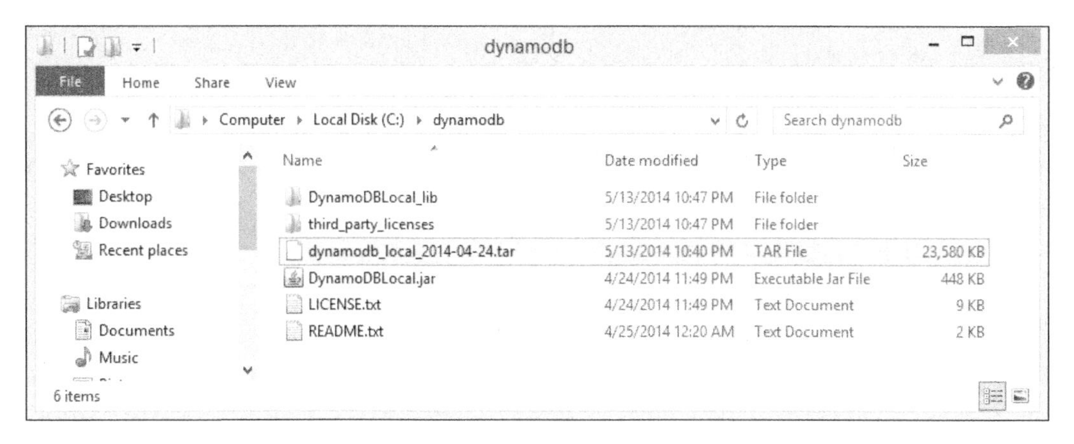

Starting the DynamoDB Local is very easy. First we need to change the working directory using the `cd` command, and then we can start DynamoDB Local on port `8888` using the following command:

```
java -D java.library.path=./DynamoDBLocal_lib -jar DynamoDBLocal.jar
-port 8888
```

Even the `java -D java.library.path = ./DynamoDBLocal_lib -jar DynamoDBLocal.jar` command is enough to start DynamoDB Local, but it starts it on port 8000, which is occupied by my PC. That's why I use port 8888.

Once you put in this command from the CLI, you will get the following output:

```
Command Prompt - java -Djava.library.path=./DynamoDBLocal_lib -jar Dynamo...
Microsoft Windows [Version 6.2.9200]
(c) 2012 Microsoft Corporation. All rights reserved.

C:\Users\ADMIN>cd C:\dynamodb

C:\dynamodb>java -Djava.library.path=./DynamoDBLocal_lib -jar DynamoDBLocal.jar
-port 8888
2014-05-18 23:21:12.855:INFO:oejs.Server:jetty-8.1.12.v20130726
2014-05-18 23:21:12.945:INFO:oejs.AbstractConnector:Started SelectChannelConnect
or@0.0.0.0:8888
```

Once DynamoDB Local starts, it's easier to configure the client. We need to make changes in three lines of our `initializeCredentials` method (we have discussed this in the *Java SDK operations* section in this chapter). We need to insert a new line pointing to the DynamoDB Local host and port using the `client.setEndpoint()` method (as shown next). Then we need to remove other client-related setters such as `setRegion`. Take a look at the following code:

```
private static void initializeCredentials() throws Exception {
  AWSCredentials credentials = null;
  try {
    credentials = new ProfileCredentialsProvider()
      .getCredentials();
  } catch (Exception e) {
    thrownew AmazonClientException(
    "Invalid location or format of credentials file.",e);
  }
  client = new AmazonDynamoDBClient(credentials);
  client.setEndpoint("http://localhost:8888");
  //Region usWest2 = Region.getRegion(Regions.US_WEST_2);
  //client.setRegion(usWest2);
}
```

After this, if we run the `AwsSdkDemo` class it will give the following output in the console (where DynamoDB Local starts):

```
Command Prompt - java -Djava.library.path=./DynamoDBLocal_lib -jar Dynamo...
Microsoft Windows [Version 6.2.9200]
(c) 2012 Microsoft Corporation. All rights reserved.

C:\Users\ADMIN>cd C:\dynamodb

C:\dynamodb>java -Djava.library.path=./DynamoDBLocal_lib -jar DynamoDBLocal.jar
-port 8888
2014-05-18 23:21:12.855:INFO:oejs.Server:jetty-8.1.12.v20130726
2014-05-18 23:21:12.945:INFO:oejs.AbstractConnector:Started SelectChannelConnect
or@0.0.0.0:8888
May 18, 2014 11:25:27 PM com.almworks.sqlite4java.Internal log
INFO: [sqlite] DB[1]: instantiated [AKIAIJAN5EPLHLEGAK3A_us-east-1.db]
May 18, 2014 11:25:27 PM com.almworks.sqlite4java.Internal log
INFO: [sqlite] Internal: loaded sqlite4java-win32-x64 from C:\dynamodb\DynamoDBL
ocal_lib\sqlite4java-win32-x64.dll
May 18, 2014 11:25:27 PM com.almworks.sqlite4java.Internal log
INFO: [sqlite] Internal: loaded sqlite 3.7.10, wrapper 0.2
May 18, 2014 11:25:27 PM com.almworks.sqlite4java.Internal log
INFO: [sqlite] DB[1]: opened
```

DynamoDB Local stores all this data in a local SQLite database.

Summary

In this chapter, we have learned how to create an SDK project and how to perform SDK operations. Moreover, we have seen how DynamoDB Local works at client side. From DynamoDB Local we can understand the behavior of the DynamoDB database at the local end.

Indexes are very important for any database. So in the next chapter, we will learn what secondary indexes are, how to use secondary indexes with DynamoDB, and how they work effectively in DynamoDB.

4
Working with Secondary Indexes

In the previous chapter, we saw how to work with DynamoDB SDK. We discussed table creation, item insertion, and updating a table using Java SDK. During table creation, we used two functions to create the local and global secondary indexes that we will discuss now.

Projection helps the programmer to decide which attributes have to be added to the secondary index.

Understanding the secondary index and projections should go hand in hand because of the fact that a secondary index cannot be used efficiently without specifying projection. In this chapter, we will cover the following topics:

- Global secondary indexes
- Local secondary indexes
- Projection
- Item sharding
- Best practices

The use of projection in DynamoDB is pretty much similar to that of traditional databases. Before learning about projection, go through *Chapter 2, DynamoDB Interfaces*, and *Chapter 3, Tools and Libraries of AWS DynamoDB*, which deal with the DynamoDB data model where we use some basics of secondary indexes. These chapters deal with a little theory behind DynamoDB secondary indexes, which is pretty important for starting with projection.

For those who don't want to go through both the chapters, here are a few things to watch out for:

- Whenever a DynamoDB table is created, it is mandatory to create a primary key, which can be of a simple type (hash type), or it can be of a complex type (hash and range key).
- For the specified primary key, an index will be created (we call this index the primary index).
- Along with this primary key index, the user is allowed to create up to five secondary indexes per table.
- There are two kinds of secondary index. The first is a local secondary index (in which the hash key of the index must be the same as that of the table) and the second is the global secondary index (in which the hash key can be any field). In both of these secondary index types, the range key can be a field that the user needs to create an index for.

Secondary indexes

A quick question: while writing a query in any database, keeping the primary key field as part of the query (especially in the `where` condition) will return results much faster compared to the other way. Why? This is because of the fact that an index will be created automatically in most of the databases for the primary key field. This is the case with DynamoDB also. This index is called the primary index of the table. There is no customization possible using the primary index, so the primary index is seldom discussed.

In order to make retrieval faster, the frequently-retrieved attributes need to be made as part of the index. However, a DynamoDB table can have only one primary index and the index can have a maximum of two attributes (hash and range key). So for faster retrieval, the user should be given privileges to create user-defined indexes. This index, which is created by the user, is called the secondary index. Similar to the table key schema, the secondary index also has a key schema. Based on the key schema attributes, the secondary index can be either a local or global secondary index. Whenever a secondary index is created, during every item insertion, the items in the index will be rearranged. This rearrangement will happen for each item insertion into the table, provided the item contains both the index's hash and range key attribute.

Projection

Once we have an understanding of the secondary index, we are all set to learn about projection. While creating the secondary index, it is mandatory to specify the hash and range attributes, based on which the index is created. Apart from these two attributes, if the query wants one or more attribute (assuming that none of these attributes are projected into the index), then DynamoDB will scan the entire table. This will consume a lot of throughput capacity and will have comparatively higher latency.

The following is the table (with some data) that is used to store book information:

BookTitle	Author	Publisher	PubDate	Language	Edition	Author2
SCJP	Kathy Sierra	Tata Mcgraw	28-Dec-08	English	1	Bert Bates
SCJP	Khalid A. Mughal	Dorling Kindersley	14-Mar-09	English	3	Rolf W. Rasmussen
SCJP	Richard F. Raposa	Wiley India	19-Jan-09	English	4	
Inferno	Dan Brown	Doubleday	14-May-13	English	1	
Let us C	Yashwant Kanetkar	BPB	13-Apr-10	English	2	

Table 4.1 - Table Tbl_Book with sample data

Here are few more details about the table:

- The `BookTitle` attribute is the hash key of the table and local secondary index
- The `Edition` attribute is the range key of the table
- The `PubDate` attribute is the range key of the index (let's call this index `IDX_PubDate`)

Local secondary index

While creating the secondary index, the hash and range key of the table and index will be inserted into the index; optionally, the user can specify what other attributes need to be added. There are three kinds of projection possible in DynamoDB:

- `KEYS_ONLY`: Using this, the index consists of the hash and range key values of the table and index
- `INCLUDE`: Using this, the index consists of attributes in `KEYS_ONLY` plus other non-key attributes that we specify
- `ALL`: Using this, the index consists of all of the attributes from the source table

The following code shows the creation of a local secondary index named `Idx_PubDate` with `BookTitle` as the hash key (which is a must in the case of a local secondary index), `PubDate` as the range key, and using the `KEYS_ONLY` projection:

```
private static LocalSecondaryIndex getLocalSecondaryIndex() {
  ArrayList<KeySchemaElement> indexKeySchema =
    newArrayList<KeySchemaElement>();
  indexKeySchema.add(new KeySchemaElement()
    .withAttributeName("BookTitle")
    .withKeyType(KeyType.HASH));
  indexKeySchema.add(new KeySchemaElement()
    .withAttributeName("PubDate")
    .withKeyType(KeyType.RANGE));
  LocalSecondaryIndex lsi = new LocalSecondaryIndex()
    .withIndexName("Idx_PubDate")
    .withKeySchema(indexKeySchema)
    .withProjection(new Projection()
    .withProjectionType("KEYS_ONLY"));
  return lsi;
}
```

The usage of the `KEYS_ONLY` index type will create the smallest possible index and the usage of `ALL` will create the biggest possible index. We will discuss the trade-offs between these index types a little later.

Going back to our example, let us assume that we are using the `KEYS_ONLY` index type, so none of the attributes (other than the previous three key attributes) are projected into the index. So the index will look as follows:

BookTitle	PubDate	Edition
SCJP	28-Dec-2008	1
SCJP	19-Jan-2009	4
SCJP	14-Mar-2009	3
Inferno	14-May-13	1
Let us C	13-Apr-10	2

Table 4.2 - Table showing the contents of index

> You may notice that the row order of the index is almost the same as that of the table order (except the second and third rows. Here, you can observe one point: the table records will be grouped primarily based on the hash key, and then the records that have the same hash key will be ordered based on the range key of the index. In the case of the index, even though the table's range key is part of the index attribute, it will not play any role in the ordering. (only the index's hash and range keys will take part in the ordering).

There is a negative to this approach. If the user is writing a query using this index to fetch `BookTitle` and `Publisher` with `PubDate` as `28-Dec-2008`, then what happens? Will DynamoDB complain that the `Publisher` attribute is not projected into the index? The answer is no. The reason is that even though `Publisher` is not projected into the index, we can still retrieve it using the secondary index. We will discuss the scan and query operations in detail in *Chapter 5, Query and Scan Operations in DynamoDB*. However, retrieving a nonprojected attribute will scan the entire table. So if we are sure that certain attributes need to be fetched frequently, then we must project it into the index; otherwise, it will consume a large number of capacity units and retrieval will be much slower as well.

One more question: if the user is writing a query using the local secondary index to fetch `BookTitle` and `Publisher` with `PubDate` as `28-Dec-2008`, then what happens? Will DynamoDB complain that the `PubDate` attribute is not part of the primary key and hence queries are not allowed on nonprimary key attributes? The answer is no. It is a rule of thumb that we can write queries on the secondary index attributes. It is possible to include nonprimary key attributes as part of the query, but these attributes must at least be key attributes of the index.

The following code shows how to add non-key attributes to the secondary index's projection:

```
private static Projection getProjectionWithNonKeyAttr() {
  Projection projection = new Projection()
    .withProjectionType(ProjectionType.INCLUDE);
  ArrayList<String> nonKeyAttributes = new ArrayList<String>();
  nonKeyAttributes.add("Language");
  nonKeyAttributes.add("Author2");
  projection.setNonKeyAttributes(nonKeyAttributes);
  return projection;
}
```

There is a slight limitation with the local secondary index. If we write a query on a non-key (both table and index) attribute, then internally DynamoDB might need to scan the entire table; this is inefficient. For example, consider a situation in which we need to retrieve the number of editions of the books in each and every language. Since both of the attributes are non-key, even if we create a local secondary index with either of the attributes (`Edition` and `Language`), the query will still result in a scan operation on the entire table.

Global secondary index

A problem arises here: is there any way in which we can create a secondary index using both the index keys that are different from the table's primary keys? The answer is the global secondary index. The following code shows how to create the global secondary index for this scenario:

```
private static GlobalSecondaryIndex getGlobalSecondaryIndex() {
  GlobalSecondaryIndex gsi = new GlobalSecondaryIndex()
    .withIndexName("Idx_Pub_Edtn")
    .withProvisionedThroughput(new ProvisionedThroughput()
    .withReadCapacityUnits((long) 1)
    .withWriteCapacityUnits((long) 1))
    .withProjection(newProjection().withProjectionType
      ("KEYS_ONLY"));

  ArrayList<KeySchemaElement> indexKeySchema1 =
    newArrayList<KeySchemaElement>();

  indexKeySchema1.add(new KeySchemaElement()
    .withAttributeName("Language")
    .withKeyType(KeyType.HASH));
  indexKeySchema1.add(new KeySchemaElement()
    .withAttributeName("Edition")
    .withKeyType(KeyType.RANGE));

  gsi.setKeySchema(indexKeySchema1);
  return gsi;
}
```

While deciding the attributes to be projected into a global secondary index, there are trade-offs we must consider between provisioned throughput and storage costs. A few of these are listed as follows:

- If our application doesn't need to query a table so often and it performs frequent writes or updates against the data in the table, then we must consider projecting the `KEYS_ONLY` attributes. The global secondary index will be the minimum size, but it will still be available when required for the query activity.

- The smaller the index, the cheaper the cost to store it and our write costs will be cheaper too. If we need to access only those few attributes that have the lowest possible latency, then we must project only those (lesser) attributes into a global secondary index.
- If we need to access almost all of the non-key attributes of the DynamoDB table on a frequent basis, we can project these attributes (even the entire table) into the global secondary index. This will give us maximum flexibility with the trade-off that our storage cost would increase, or even double if we project the entire table's attributes into the index.
- The additional storage costs to store the global secondary index might equalize the cost of performing frequent table scans. If our application will frequently retrieve some non-key attributes, we must consider projecting these non-key attributes into the global secondary index.

Item sharding

Sharding, also called horizontal partitioning, is a technique in which rows are distributed among the database servers to perform queries faster. In the case of sharding, a hash operation will be performed on the table rows (mostly on one of the columns) and, based on the hash operation output, the rows will be grouped and sent to the proper database server. Take a look at the following diagram:

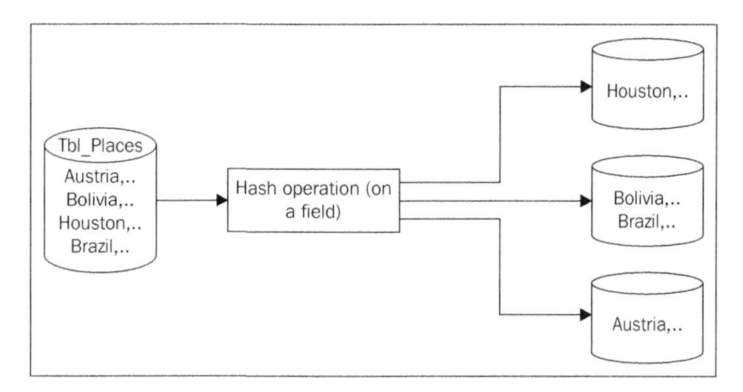

As shown in the previous diagram, if all the table data (only four rows and one column are shown for illustration purpose) is stored in a single database server, the read and write operations will become slower and the server that has the frequently accessed table data will work more compared to the server storing the table data that is not accessed frequently.

The following diagram shows the advantage of sharding over a multitable, multiserver database environment:

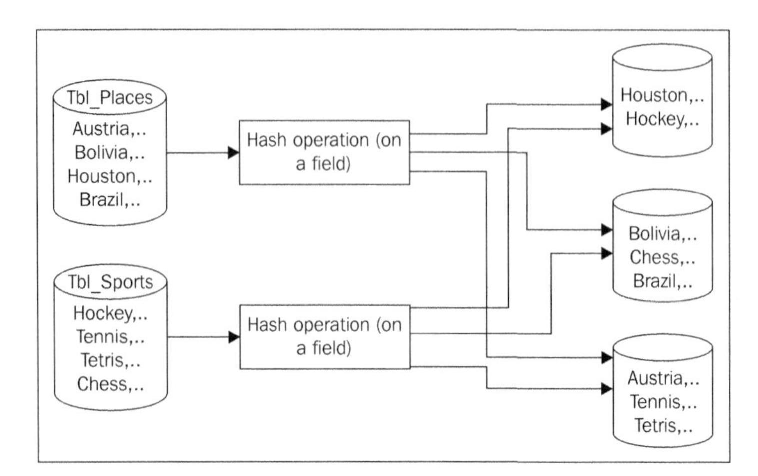

In the previous diagram, two tables (**Tbl_Places** and **Tbl_Sports**) are shown on the left-hand side with four sample rows of data (**Austria..** means only the first column of the first item is illustrated and all other fields are represented by **..**).We are going to perform a hash operation on the first column only. In DynamoDB, this hashing will be performed automatically. Once the hashing is done, similar hash rows will be saved automatically in different servers (if necessary) to satisfy the specified provisioned throughput capacity.

While discussing the hash type key (primary key and index) in earlier chapters, have you ever wondered about the importance of the hash type key while creating a table (which is mandatory)? Of course we all know the importance of the range key and what it does. It simply sorts items based on the range key value. So far, we might have been thinking that the range key is more important than the hash key. If you think that way, then you may be correct, provided we neither need our table to be provisioned faster nor do we need to create any partitions for our table. As long as the table data is smaller, the importance of the hash key will be realized only while writing a query operation. However, once the table grows, in order to satisfy the same provision throughput, DynamoDB needs to partition our table data based on this hash key (as shown in the previous diagram).

This partitioning of table items based on the hash key attribute is called sharding. It means the partitions are created by splitting items and not attributes. This is the reason why a query that has the hash key (of table and index) retrieves items much faster.

Since the number of partitions is managed automatically by DynamoDB, we cannot just hope for things to work fine. We also need to keep certain things in mind, for example, the hash key attribute should have more distinct values. To simplify, it is not advisable to put binary values (such as `Yes` or `No`, `Present` or `Past` or `Future`, and so on) into the hash key attributes, thereby restricting the number of partitions. If our hash key attribute has either `Yes` or `No` values in all the items, then DynamoDB can create only a maximum of two partitions; therefore, the specified provisioned throughput cannot be achieved.

Just consider that we have created a table called `Tbl_Sports` with a provisioned throughput capacity of 10, and then we put 10 items into the table. Assuming that only a single partition is created, we are able to retrieve 10 items per second. After a point of time, we put 10 more items into the table. DynamoDB will create another partition (by hashing over the hash key), thereby satisfying the provisioned throughput capacity. There is a formula taken from the AWS site:

Total provisioned throughput/partitions = throughput per partition

OR

No. of partitions = Total provisioned throughput/throughput per partition

In order to satisfy throughput capacity, the other parameters will be automatically managed by DynamoDB.

Ideal item writing

We will write the following data into `Tbl_Book`, which we have discussed in earlier chapters:

Attribute	BookTitle	Author	Publisher	PubDate	Language	Edition	Author2
Type	**Hash**	**Range**	**Optional attributes**				
Item1	SCJP	Kathy	TMH		English	1	Bert Bates
Item2-1000	SCJP	999 Items with different Author (range key) and other attributes					
Item1001	Let us C	Kanetkar			English		
Item1002-2000	Let us C	999 Items with different Author (range key) and other attributes					
Item2001	Hadoop	Tom White		28-Dec-09	English		
Item2002-3000	Hadoop	999 Items with different Author (range key) and other attributes					

Table 4.3 - Table showing sample 3000 items available in Tbl_Book

As we can see, there is a total of 3,000 book details available. Even though only three unique book titles, namely SCJP, Let us C, and Hadoop, are available in the data, the range key (Author) is different. So there are 1,000 different authors for the same book title. The first 1000 items, that is Item1 to Item1000, have information about the SCJP book (with 1000 different and unique authors) and so on.

As we already discussed horizontal partitioning and that it is done on the hash attribute, let's assume that three partitions will be created for storing this table data. One of the partitions will store the SCJP books, the other will store Hadoop, and the third one will store Let us C. The question is, which of the following insertions is suitable for working with DynamoDB?

- The insertion order based on item order, that is, Item1, Item2, and Item3 through Item3000
- The insertion order based on round-robin on the hash key, that is, Item1, then Item1001, then Item2001, then Item1002, and so on

I hope you got the difference between the two insertions.

The first method is not advised and the second is most suitable. Before discussing the reason, let's explore how this insertion works internally. The first insertion method will insert the items into first partition and then to the second partition, and so on. So, it overloads one partition with too many writes (insertions). During that time, the other two partitions will be idle. That is the reason why the first insertion method is not ideal or the correct way of using the DynamoDB put item. So we must follow the second approach, which will distribute the write requests uniformly across partitions.

> Even though in our data we have only three unique hash attribute values (SCJP, Hadoop, and Let us C), these kinds of binary and ternary hash values are not advised for DynamoDB (this is discussed in the *Item sharding* section of this chapter).

Therefore, because of sharding (or horizontal partitioning), DynamoDB partitions not only the table but also the index associated with the table, so the read requests will be faster.

Best practices with secondary indexes

There are four rules to create the secondary index so that our table will function without any hiccups. These rules are as follows:

- Distributing the load by choosing the correct key
- Making use of the sparse index
- Using the global secondary index for quicker retrieval
- Creating a read replica

Distributing the load by choosing the correct key

In the case of a multipartition table, the data as well as the table's associated indexes will be distributed across servers. This distribution of indexes across servers is determined by the value of one of the attributes of the index. Yes, you're correct: it is decided by the hash key value. *Unlike the hash key value (compounded with the range key) of a table, indexes keys can be duplicated.* In the case of local secondary indexes, this problem will not occur because of the fact that the table's hash key is the same as that of the index, so the index will be distributed similar to the table. Therefore, this practice must be kept in mind while designing a global secondary index.

For example, let's take a look at the global secondary index `Idx_Pub_Edtn` created by us at the start of this chapter. In this index, we set the `Language` attribute as the hash key and the `Edition` attribute as the range key, so the index will be distributed based on the value of the `Language` attribute.

If we assume that our table has books written only in four different languages (English, German, Latin, and Greek), each server or partition (assuming that four partitions are created for this table) holds details about the book written in each language. As we are aware that most of the books will be written in English, the number of books written in other languages will be fewer, so, the server storing books in the English language will perform (and handle) too many read and write requests compared to other languages. This is called skewed data. Therefore, we need to avoid these kinds of indexes that will make our retrieval slower. Can we make the `Edition` attribute as the hash key and the `Language` attribute as the range key of the global secondary index? I will give you a hint about the table. As we all know, most of the books will not make it to the second edition.

Making use of the sparse index

While inserting an item into the DynamoDB table, we must specify the primary key attributes, but it is not mandatory for an item to have the secondary attributes. If an item doesn't contain secondary index attributes, then the item will not be available in the secondary index.

BookTitle	Author	Publisher	PubDate	Language	Edition	Author2
SCJP	Kathy Sierra	Tata Mcgraw	28-Dec-08	English	1	Bert Bates
SCJP	Khalid A. Mughal	Dorling Kindersley	14-Mar-09	English	3	Rolf W. Rasmussen
SCJP	Richard F. Raposa	Wiley India	19-Jan-09	English	4	
Inferno	Dan Brown	Doubleday	14-May-13	English	1	
Let us C	Yashwant Kanetkar	BPB	13-Apr-10	English	2	

Table 4.4 - Table Tbl_Book with sample data

The previous table is the table that we use to explain the usage of sparse index. Our problem statement is to find out which author pair is more frequent. So for faster retrieval, we are going to use the global secondary index with the `Author` attribute as hash and the `Author2` attribute as the range key. The previous table has five items. Our global secondary index will have how many attributes: five or three? The answer is three. Why?

An item's attributes will be projected only if the index's key values (hash and range) are present in the item. This property is called sparse. This kind of index is called the sparse index. For these kinds of problem statements, the use of this kind of index will be beneficial for retrieval of results as well as storage and insertion.

Using the global secondary index for quicker retrieval

In the previous table, if some of the attributes are not frequently accessed (for example, `Publisher`, `PubDate`, and `Edition`), then even though these will not be part of our query, they will consume more provisioned throughput and will result in slower retrieval of data. There are two solutions available to solve this problem.

The simpler approach is to remove these rarely used attributes from the table. This will not work well in many cases because even though these attributes are rarely used, they might contain some precious information (such as `Edition`) that might be required in future. So, we need to go for the second approach: using the secondary index.

The second solution is to create an index with the same key (both hash and range) as that of the table and project only frequently used attributes into this index, without disturbing the table items and attributes. Since DynamoDB allows us to specify different provisional throughput capacity for the index, we can decide the data (read and write) speed for this index. After doing this, for quicker retrieval, we need to direct the queries directly to this index, instead of using the table for querying. This is the usage of the global secondary index for quicker retrieval.

Creating a read replica

In the initial stage of an application, the database size will be small enough to handle any number of read or write requests with high throughput speeds. However, once our application and number of users grows, the access speed problem arises. A few of the applications might be using the common table too. So, we need to direct the mission critical (or hot) requests to a place that can provide faster read/writes, and the low-priority requests can be directed to some slower read/writes (with some eventually consistent data). We will discuss about eventual consistency in the next chapter.

The solution is very simple. Create a duplicate copy of the data (called replication) by creating a global secondary index. Configure this index for very high throughput capacity compared to the other data source. Then, redirect all the mission-critical requests to this index. In this way, higher priority is given to deserving applications by keeping nondeserving applications (which neither require consistent data nor higher speed) on the back foot. This practice will handle throttled requests very well.

The previous rule applies only for global secondary indexes. Local secondary indexes have rules too, following which access to the items will be efficient. The rules are as follows:

- Use indexes sparingly
- Choose projections carefully
- Optimize frequent queries to avoid fetches
- Take advantage of sparse indexes
- Watch out for expanding item collections

Using indexes sparingly

It is not advisable to create an index for an attribute (it might be a key attribute as well as non-key attributes projected) that is frequently updated and rarely used in queries. Frequent updating of table items will update its associated index items as well. Due to this, we might suffer very high I/O cost. On the other hand, projecting (or creating an index for) rarely used attributes will make us incur a high level of storage cost. So, the index has to be created only for attributes used in queries.

In reality, most of our applications frequently add or update items into the DynamoDB table. Does that mean we cannot (efficiently) use an index for this kind of a table? There is a solution. This kind of application that frequently captures items (for example, social networking sites) is commonly called a data capture application. In the case of data capture applications, we are not supposed to create an index directly for this table. Instead we need to copy this data to another table (repeatedly over a period of time) and create an index for this newly created table. However, there is one restriction here: the read operation might not return the latest data available. For example, if the data copy operation happens every hour (the period is set to an hour) and if the last copy operation occurred at 2 p.m., the read operation performed at 2:59 p.m. will not return the items updated on the DynamoDB table. Even though this strategy doesn't return the latest data, this is suitable for applications where data consistency is tolerable for a period of time.

Choosing projections carefully

From a cost perspective, if we don't want to pay too much to DynamoDB, then we must choose the projections carefully. As long as each item size is not greater than 1 KB (1 capacity unit), even if we project all the attributes (or only the `KEY` attributes), it doesn't make any change in the billing, but the speed of retrieval will differ. So it's better to project only the attributes to be retrieved frequently using the query operation. Otherwise, a lot of time and money will be spent on I/O and storage.

Do you have the same question that I have? If we need to project only the necessary attributes into the index, then what is the use of the projection type `ALL`? There is a slight but important difference.

If the index is created with the same hash and range key (using `ALL` as the projection type), then there is no point in creating the index at all: both will function the same. Then what is the use of the index with the projection type `ALL`? It is useful only if the range key is different, otherwise it is of no use. It will consume twice the storage without doing anything.

Optimizing frequent queries to avoid fetches

Frequently used queries should return the output faster. To do this, all the attributes used in the frequent queries must be projected into the secondary index and, depending on the frequency of query usage, the provisioned throughput also has to be set. Even if one of the attributes is not projected into the index then the query will scan the entire table, which will increase the latency. However, we need to keep one thing in mind, that *occasional querying might become frequent querying sometimes, but during that time we cannot add (project) this attribute into the index.*

Watching for expanding item collections

While creating a DynamoDB table, there are no restrictions. But once it has been created, there are a few limitations. One such limitation is on the hash key limit. We already know that table items will be partitioned on the hash key value. What we don't know is that it is not possible for the same hash key value (of the table and index collectively) to have items greater than 10 GB.

For example, in our `Tbl_Book` function, we have a hash key attribute named `BookTitle`. Let's say that we inserted items with `BookTitle` as SCJP and after a point of time, we stored items with a collective size of 6 GB with SCJP as the hash key. If we create an index with `BookTitle` as the hash key (and assume that 4 GB space is consumed by the SCJP hash key in the index), we cannot insert even a single item into this table. So if a large number of items need to be inserted for certain hash key attributes, then we are not supposed to create any secondary indexes with the same hash key, which will restrict the size of the table. Beyond 10 GB, DynamoDB will start returning `ItemCollectionSizeLimitExceededException`.

Summary

In this chapter, we saw what the local and global secondary indexes are. We walked through projection and its usage with indexes. We also saw the best practices to implement and studied the use cases of secondary indexes.

In the next chapter, we will see how different types of scanning and query operations work in DynamoDB. Also, we will see how they are useful with databases.

5

Query and Scan Operations in DynamoDB

In the previous chapter, we learned to create a secondary index for a table and its role in retrieving the items efficiently. In the long run, knowledge of the secondary index is useful only if we know how to use it for retrieval. Item retrieval can be done in DynamoDB using two operations called query and scan. Similarly we also discussed sharding. In this chapter, we will learn about parallel scanning, which makes use of the sharding concept. The primary objective of any database (whether it be NoSQL or SQL) is to provide easy storage and faster retrieval of data. So far, we have discussed various configurations that can be added to our table, such as adding an index, specifying the primary key, and so on. In this chapter, we will cover the following topics:

- Querying table items
- Scanning table items
- Parallel scanning

First, we will discuss the query operation, which makes use of the hash and range key values to retrieve the items. Then we will shift our focus to the scan operation, which will scan the entire table. Finally we will discuss the limitations of (sequential) scan operations, which give rise to parallel scanning.

Querying tables

One of the most efficient ways of retrieving data from a DynamoDB table is by using the query operation on the table. One of the mandatory parameters or conditions to be provided while performing a query operation is performing a comparison operation on the primary key attribute value. The query operation supports the following comparison operations, namely:

- `EQ`: This stands for equal to
- `LE`: This stands for less than or equal to
- `LT`: This stands for less than
- `GE`: This stands for greater than or equal to
- `GT`: This stands for greater than
- `BETWEEN`: This retrieves items whose primary key value is between the specified values
- `BEGINS_WITH`: This retrieves items whose primary key begins with the specified value

These seven comparison operations can be performed directly on primary key values, which will retrieve only the necessary items (without even bothering the partitions/items that don't have this value). There are six more comparison operations that can be performed on the items, but are not directly useful in the query operation. The following operations can be used to filter the items returned by the query operation further, using it in the query filter and scan filter condition:

- `NE`: This stands for not equal to
- `IN`: This retrieves items whose attribute value in the filter is one of the specified values
- `NOT_NULL`: This retrieves items whose attribute value in the filter is not null
- `NULL`: This retrieves items whose attribute value in the filter is null
- `CONTAINS`: This retrieves items whose attribute value in the filter has a specified string
- `NOT_CONTAINS`: This returns an item whose attribute value doesn't have a specified string

There are several enhancements that could be made to the query operation. But what we are going to discuss here are the necessary and important aspects of a query. First of all we will see how a simple query looks:

```
//Creates a HASH condition equivalent to BookTitle=SCJP
Condition hashKeyCondition = new Condition()
```

```
    .withComparisonOperator(ComparisonOperator.EQ)
    .withAttributeValueList(new AttributeValue().withS("SCJP"));
  Map<String, Condition> keyConditions = new HashMap<String,
    Condition>();
  keyConditions.put("BookTitle", hashKeyCondition);
  QueryRequest queryRequest = new QueryRequest()
    .withTableName("Tbl_Book")
    .withKeyConditions(keyConditions);
  QueryResult result = client.query(queryRequest);
```

The first parameter needed for the query operation is the comparison condition. So we will create an instance of the `com.amazonaws.services.dynamodbv2.model.Condition` class. We must configure this instance with two mandatory parameters (`ComparisonOperator` and `AttributeValue` list).

The first parameter will be an instance of an enumerator available in the DynamoDB SDK package `com.amazonaws.services.dynamodbv2.model.ComparisonOperator`. Here, we have configured it with `EQ` (whose description is given in the previous code block's comment as well as at the beginning of this section).

The second parameter is the list of `com.amazonaws.services.dynamodbv2.model.AttributeValue`. In the case of `EQ`, it takes only one `AttributeValue`, which is SCJP. But, if we use `BETWEEN`, then it will take two parameters. Then we create a map called `keyConditions` of the type `Map<String, Condition>`. Then we put the hash attribute named `BookTitle` as the key and the condition instance we have configured earlier.

The previous code is the minimum parameter required to perform a query operation on a table. First, we need to create an instance of the `com.amazonaws.services.dynamodbv2.model.QueryRequest` (or the latest version) class, and then, to that instance, we need to add a few mandatory configuration details such as table name, and optional details such as index name, scan filter, and so on (which we will discuss later).

Once the `QueryRequest` instance is configured, we can invoke the query method available with `DynamoDBClient` (just as we invoked the `createTable` method to create the table) by enclosing the `QueryRequest` instance. The query operation will return an instance of the `com.amazonaws.services.dynamodbv2.model.QueryResult` class. We can use the `getItems()` method available with the `QueryResult` instance, which will return a `List<Map<String, AttributeValue>>`. We can iterate this list to fetch the attribute name and value.

Querying a secondary index is not much different from the earlier code. All we need to do is add `.withIndexName("Idx_Pub_Edtn")` to the `QueryRequest` instance, where `Idx_Pub_edtn` is the name of the index.

The previous code will return all the items whose hash key attribute value `BookTitle` equals SCJP. Since the range key is also part of the primary key, we can add the range key condition to the `QueryRequest` instance (along with the hash key condition). We need to add the following lines to the previous code block:

```
//Creates a RANGE condition equivalent to PubDate > 1989-12-28
Condition rangeKeyCondition = new Condition()
  .withComparisonOperator(ComparisonOperator.GT.toString())
  .withAttributeValueList(new AttributeValue()
  .withS("1989-12-28"));
keyConditions.put("PubDate", rangeKeyCondition);
```

We can put (or add) this range key condition to the key condition map, which is already added to the `QueryRequest` instance (in the first code block). Now, the query will return the items matching both conditions. Since the `date` data type is not there in DynamoDB, the comparison will be performed as a string comparison. That is the reason why we chose the date format as `yyyy-MM-dd` instead of other formats.

If we store the `PubDate` attribute in the same `dd-MMM-yyyy` format (used in the earlier chapters), then the `GT` and `LT` operations will not yield the predicted output because the comparison operation here is performed as a string comparison (and not as a date string).

Along with these two primary key conditions, several other add-ons are available for configuring the query. Let me name these one by one:

- Usage of the exclusive start key
- Usage of the query or scan filter
- Usage of limit
- Usage of `Select` to retrieve only specified parameters using the `AttributesToGet` list
- Usage of consistency
- Usage of index and scanning direction

We will discuss each of these in detail. The first four configurations are common to both query and scan operations, and the next two configurations are available only for query. Let's first see how these could be added to the `QueryRequest` instance. Then we will discuss detailed configurations. Have a look at the following code:

```
QueryRequest queryRequest = new QueryRequest()
  .withTableName("Tbl_Book")
  .withKeyConditions(keyConditions)
  .withIndexName("Index_Name")
  .withScanIndexForward(true)
  .withSelect(Select.SPECIFIC_ATTRIBUTES)
  .withAttributesToGet(Arrays.asList("BookTitle", "PubDate"))
  .withLimit(10)
  .withConsistentRead(true);
```

We are already familiar with the first two (`with`) methods, which configure the table name and key conditions to the `QueryRequest` instance. The third parameter specifies the index through which the query has to be executed. The fourth parameter specifies whether the search (or query operation) on index should be retrieved in the ascending order; `true` means ascending order, `false` means descending order. By default, the ordering is ascending.

The fifth parameter is used to tell `QueryRequest`, which are all the attributes that need to be retrieved from the table. `Select` is an enumerator just like `ComparisonOperator`, whose possible values are shown as follows:

- `ALL_ATTRIBUTES`: This returns all the item attributes from the table or index.
- `ALL_PROJECTED_ATTRIBUTES`: This returns all the item attributes from the index and does not apply to the table. If all the table attributes are projected into the secondary index, then `ALL_PROJECTED_ATTRIBUTES` will function in the same way as `ALL_ATTRIBUTES`.
- `SPECIFIC_ATTRIBUTES`: This returns the attributes specified in the `AttributesToGet` list, which is the sixth parameter in our `QueryRequest`.
- `COUNT`: This returns the number of matching items.

The sixth parameter (as discussed) takes `String[]` or `List<String>` with the attribute names that are to be retrieved by the query operation. The seventh parameter limits the number of items to be retrieved by the query. This is usually used along with the exclusive start key (which we will discuss later). The last parameter is used to specify whether the read has to be strongly consistent.

Consistency

Before discussing the eighth parameter used to configure a query, we must learn about DynamoDB's consistency model. There are two kinds of consistency models in DynamoDB, which are listed as follows:

- Eventually consistent
- Strongly consistent

These two consistency models are there in almost all the databases that comply with the ACID properties. As far as DynamoDB is concerned, it obeys the laws of the ACID properties. It gives the user the option to choose which property we want and which we don't want. DynamoDB is a distributed and redundant database. So the data is stored in multiple servers (remember sharding and partitioning) for faster access, and the same data is stored in multiple servers for a redundant purpose.

Even if one of the servers is down due to some failure, our applications (using the DynamoDB database) are still backed up by backup servers. Consistency is a measure that tells us how the update is propagated to each server holding the redundant copy of the same data.

In the case of strong consistency, the read request followed (within a very short duration) by the write request must (and will) give the updated items. The update (or insertion or deletion of an item) is propagated to each server and only then are the read operations given access to this data. No implicit locking is involved in DynamoDB. However, the user can decide on this, which we will discuss in *Chapter 7, Distributed Locking with DynamoDB*.

In the case of eventual consistency, the data returned by the query operation will be the data that was consistent in the past. So a read request followed (within a very short duration) by the write request might not give the updated items, it might still give the old data that was consistent in the past. It will take a little time for the update to propagate to every server, but eventual consistency consumes less units than strong consistency.

To be exact, strong consistency will eat up twice the number of units compared to eventual consistency. So in the case of low priority applications, where the data consistency can be compromised (to some extent), the usage of eventual consistency is economical and efficient.

If `QueryRequest` is set to `withConsistentRead(true)`, then this query will be performed with a strongly consistent read. If it is set to `false`, then the query will be performed with eventual consistency.

The query operation will help us to refine items only on primary key attributes (hash and range). In order to filter the query further, we make use of the query filter.

The following code will create a query filter returning items with `Edition` equals to `1`; usually this query filter will be used on non-key attributes.

```
//Creates a QueryFilter condition equivalent to Edition = 1
Map<String,Condition> queryFilter = new
  HashMap<String,Condition>();
  queryFilter.put("Edition", new Condition()
    .withComparisonOperator("EQ")
    .withAttributeValueList(
      new AttributeValue().withN("1")));
```

The previous code block is exactly the same as the following code block except for the syntax; both the code blocks will only create a query filter.

```
//Creates QueryFilterCondition condition equivalent to Edition = 1
Condition queryFilterCondition = new Condition()
  .withComparisonOperator(ComparisonOperator.EQ)
  .withAttributeValueList(new AttributeValue().withS("1"));
Map<String, Condition>queryFilter = new HashMap<String,
  Condition>();
queryFilter.put("Edition", queryFilterCondition);
```

The following code creates a query filter with the `Edition` condition equaling `1`; further information about `hashKeyCondition` and `rangeKeyCondition` is shown in the comments.

```
//Create a HASH key-condition equivalent to BookTitle=SCJP
//Create a RANGE key-condition equivalent to PubDate > 1989-12-28
Map<String, Condition> keyCndtns = new HashMap<String,
  Condition>();
  keyCndtns.put("BookTitle", hashKeyCondition);
  keyCndtns.put("PubDate", rangeKeyCondition);
//Creates a QueryFilter condition equivalent to Edition = 1
Map<String,Condition> queryFilter = new HashMap<String,Condition>();
  queryFilter.put("Edition", new Condition()
    .withComparisonOperator("EQ")
    .withAttributeValueList(
      new AttributeValue().withN("1")));
```

Exclusive start key

A query request always returns only 1 MB of data at a time. To fetch more data, there is a strategy available using the exclusive start key.

One of the most important concepts for the `ScanRequest` operation is the usage of the exclusive start key. But the same could be used in `QueryRequest` too. Usually, whenever we use the exclusive start key, it is mandatory to use the limit parameter. Only two new parameters (the other three parameters are already discussed) are configured to `QueryRequest`.

- The `withQueryFilter()` method is used to set the query filter map to the query request
- The last method, `withExclusiveStartKey()`, is used to notify the `QueryRequest` instance about the key of the item evaluated at present

If we observe the `do... while` loop closely, we see that we submit the `QueryRequest` instance for every ten items retrieved. For example, if 95 items satisfy both the key and query filter conditions, then this loop will be executed 10 times. During the first execution, `lastEvaluatedKey` will be null. During the second iteration `lastEvaluatedKey` will be the tenth item. During the tenth iteration, it will again become null. Have a look at the following code:

```
Map<String, AttributeValue> lastEvaluatedKey = null;
  do {
    QueryRequest queryRequest = new QueryRequest()
      .withTableName("Tbl_Book")
      .withKeyConditions(keyCndtns)
      .withQueryFilter(queryFilter)
      .withLimit(10)
      .withExclusiveStartKey(lastEvaluatedKey);
    QueryResult result = client.query(queryRequest);
    lastEvaluatedKey = result.getLastEvaluatedKey();
  }
  while (lastEvaluatedKey != null);
```

As soon as the query request is submitted, it will return only (a maximum of) ten items at a time. While executing the loop for the second time, the last evaluated item's (tenth item's) key will decide the entry point for this query request. So the second `QueryRequest` will exclude the items till the tenth item, whose key value is available in the `lastEvaluatedKey` variable.

> Usually, the limit value will be set in multiples of (at least) hundreds. This is because if the number is too small, then the number of requests to DynamoDB will be very high, due to which the item might be returned slowly if the network bandwidth is very low and the loop execution time might also result in a bottleneck.

Scanning tables

A scan operation evaluates each and every item in the table. Usually, it retrieves every item (with all the attributes along with all the items) of the table. This is the reason why the scan operation is not preferred. It is always recommended that you use query whenever possible. However, it is possible for us to retrieve only specific attributes using the `AttributesToGet` parameter, similar to the way we saw with query. Additionally, we can filter the number of items retrieved by the scan using the scan filter condition. For instance, if we assume that there are 100 items available in the table, and if the scan filter filters out 10 items using strong consistent read (which consumes a maximum of 1 KB capacity units per item), can you tell how many capacity units were eaten up by this scan operation? If you think it consumes 100 capacity units, then you're in the right boat, because the capacity unit is not a measure of how many items (hoping that every item is less than 1 KB in size) are returned, it is the measure of how many items were evaluated or scanned. So even if all the items were filtered out by the scan operation, or all items passed through the scan operation, it consumes the same number of capacity units.

First of all, we see how a simple scan looks:

```
ScanRequest scanRequest = new ScanRequest()
  .withTableName("Tbl_Book");
ScanResult result = client.scan(scanRequest);
```

The previous code is the minimum parameter required to perform a scan operation on a table. First, we need to create an instance of the `com.amazonaws.services.dynamodbv2.model.ScanRequest` (or latest) class, and then to that instance, we need to add a few mandatory configuration details, such as table name, and optional details, such as index name, scan filter, and so on (which we will discuss later).

Once the `ScanRequest` instance is configured, we can invoke the scan method available with `DynamoDBClient` (just as we invoked the `createTable` method to create a table) enclosing the `ScanRequest` instance. The scan operation will return an instance of `com.amazonaws.services.dynamodbv2.model.ScanResult`.

The scan request gives the result as pages, each with 1 MB of data. This is called pagination. In order to retrieve the next 1 MB of data, we need to execute the scan request again. This is where the exclusive start key is useful. The `ScanResult` class has a method called `getItems()` that will return a list of type `Map<String, AttributeValue>`.

We can iterate this list to fetch the attribute name and value. Most of the operations are very similar to those of a query operation. Except for two of the query operations (scanning from index and specifying the consistency), every other operation is possible in scan and with almost the same syntax.

Instead of discussing those similarities, we will spend more time on parallel scanning.

Parallel scanning

As we discussed in DynamoDB sharding, the table data is partitioned based on the hash key value. Even though this sharding will smoothen the read and write operations, it doesn't help us to scan the partitions in parallel. For example, if the table data is available in five partitions (each partition has a throughput capacity of five units), then even if the table could provision more than five capacity units, it cannot do so. The maximum throughput capacity of the table cannot exceed the fastest (having high throughput) partition. So based on these facts, what we infer is:

- A scan operation will return maximum 1 MB of data at a time
- Scan operations can read data from only one partition at a time
- For a larger table, no matter how large the throughput is, a sequential scan will always take too much time
- The scanning speed can never be faster than the fastest partition (having high throughput)

To put it simply, even if our television has one hundred channels, we will be able to see only one channel at a time.

The sequential scan works in a round robin fashion, querying no more than one partition at a time. This raises the question, is there any way by which we can perform the scan across partitions in parallel? The answer is yes. We do have a solution called parallel scanning. This parallel scanning works fine in the case of multithreading programming. We need to understand a word before proceeding with this. It is called a segment. A segment is a logical division of the table that is performed by the scan operation. We call these segment-executing threads as worker threads.

Each worker thread will issue a scan command with two parameters. The first parameter is `Segment`, which uniquely identifies the segment (usually starting from 0), and the second parameter is `TotalSegments`. All the worker threads will perform scan operations simultaneously and keep the main thread updated.

During parallel scanning, the data is segmented (based on the `TotalSegments` parameters specified while running this parallel scan).

A systematic diagram for parallel scanning is shown right after this paragraph. As per our diagram, the data is segmented into three segments (S=0, S=1, and S=2). Each segment's scan execution is taken care of by each thread, controlled by the **Application thread**.

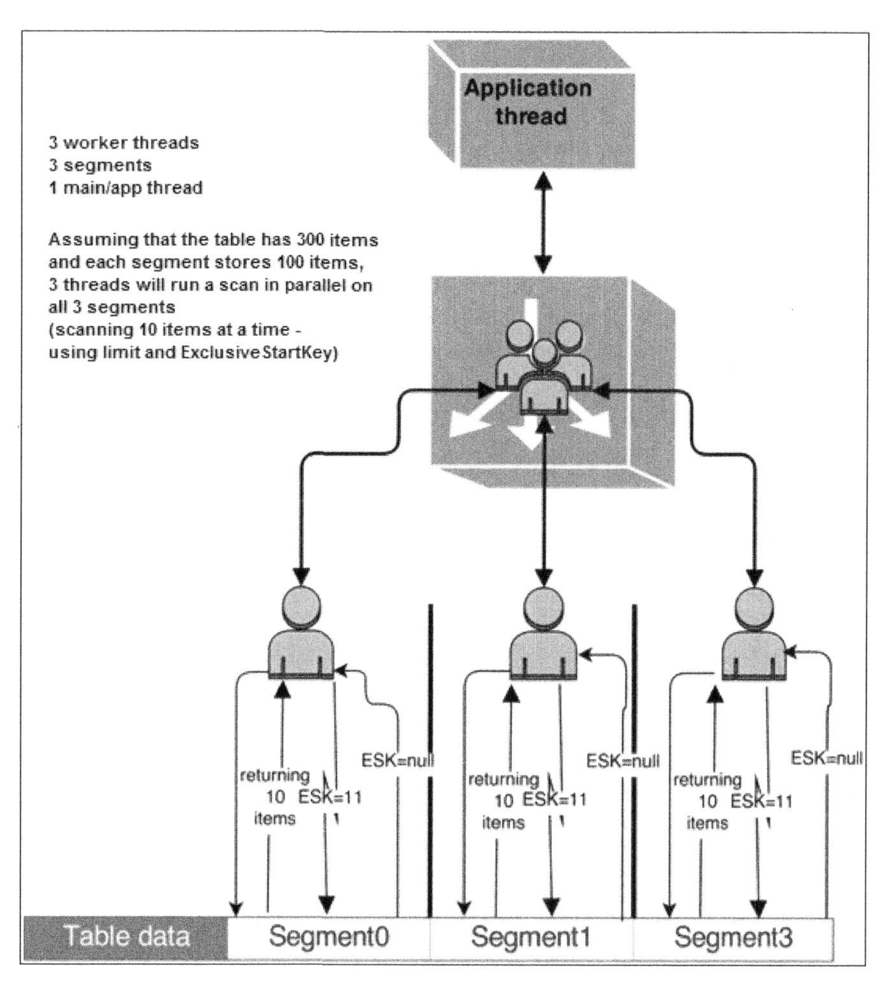

Each worker thread will return 1 MB of data queried from the segment. Do you know how it returns data to the correct worker? It identifies the worker based on the segment value (0, 1, or 2). Each worker will return the query output (each 1 MB) back to the main thread as soon as it gets the data.

It is not mandatory that the parameters (such as `Segment` and `TotalSegments`) must be the same every time we perform a parallel scan on the table. We can play with these two parameters and find out which is most suited for our requirement.

We need to keep another thing in our mind. Since three threads are scanning our table, all our throughput capacity might be used. So the `TotalSegments` parameter should not be made bigger, as it might eat up all our capacity units in one go. Therefore, for mission critical applications this approach is suitable. But, if the same approach is used by a cold application (low priority application), then critical applications sharing the same table will have to wait until the parallel scan (run by the cold application) is completed. In order to overcome this problem, we can use a limit on each worker thread scan.

Nothing in this world comes without a tradeoff. Parallel scanning does have a lot of advantages. But in the hands of an ignorant programmer, it behaves differently (mostly negatively). There are a few guidelines for better usage of (when to use) parallel scanning, which are listed as follows:

- The table size is larger (than 20 GB)
- The scan operations are not able to utilize the table's full read throughput
- A normal scan operation is very slow

These bullets will tell us whether we need parallel scanning. Once it is confirmed that we must use parallel scanning, then the second question is how could we optimize parallel scanning? The answer is as follows: if we optimize a single parameter, then our parallel scanning will work fine. The parameter that decides the number of threads is `TotalSegments`.

We should choose the optimal value for this parameter. This value can be decided only by experience, by trying several values and finding out which value suits us better. There are a few guidelines put forward by AWS, which are available in the DynamoDB documentation too. We will discuss the same guidelines here.

First and foremost, we will use parallel scanning only if our table size is above 20 GB (first guideline). So a single worker will perform the scan operation for every 2 GB of data. This means that the number of workers (which is decided by and is same as that of `TotalSegments`) will be the DynamoDB table size in GB divided by two. This will provide the optimal `TotalSegments` parameter. This is the first formula.

Secondly, we can increase the `TotalSegments` parameter from 1 through to 4096 gradually; 1 the is minimum (and a better number to start with) and 4096 is the maximum. But after increasing this number (every increment and every digit) we must make sure that none of the other applications are stared of their resources. If we feel like other applications are waiting for this parallel scan to end, then we must decrease this segment count.

There are a few clients (through which we have written multithreaded program for parallel scanning) that don't support these many threads. So we need to keep this in our mind too.

The best way of running a parallel scan is letting multiple worker threads run in parallel, but with low priority, so that other processes and applications will not get affected.

Let's get our hands dirty by visualizing parallel scanning using Java SDK. The first objective is to create a class to write the code for parallel scanning, implementing the `Runnable` interface. This class has only two methods. The first method is the parameterized constructor initializing the instance variables. The variable explanation can be referred to as follows:

- `client`: This initializes the DynamoDB client-related properties, such as AWS credentials, and so on
- `itemLimit`: This is the maximum number of items to be retrieved by a single scan request
- `totalSegments`: This is the integer specifying the number of segments to be created for this table scan
- `segment`: This initializes the segment number running this thread

To understand the variables and their working, go through the following code:

```
public class ParallelScanner implements Runnable{
  private AmazonDynamoDBClient client;
  private int itemLimit;
  private int totalSegments;
  private int segment;
  public ParallelScanner(AmazonDynamoDBClient client,
    int itemLimit, int totalSegments, int segment) {
    this.client = client;
    this.itemLimit = itemLimit;
    this.totalSegments = totalSegments;
    this.segment = segment;
  }
```

```
@Override
void run() {
  Map<String, AttributeValue> exclusiveStartKey = null;
  try {
    while(true) {
      ScanRequest scanRequest = new ScanRequest()
        .withTableName("Tbl_Book")
        .withLimit(itemLimit)
        .withExclusiveStartKey(exclusiveStartKey)
        .withTotalSegments(totalSegments)
        .withSegment(segment);
    ScanResult result = client.scan(scanRequest);
    //Use result.getItems()to print or process scan result
    exclusiveStartKey = result.getLastEvaluatedKey();
    if (exclusiveStartKey == null)
      break;
  }
 } catch (AmazonServiceException ase) {
   System.out.println(ase.getMessage());
 }
}}
```

The second method is the abstract method (run) available in the `Runnable` interface. We need to write the scanning-related requests inside this method. Inside this method, we configure our `ScanRequest` instance with values initialized in the constructor using corresponding methods. We can retrieve the output of every `ScanRequest` using the `getItems()` method available in the `ScanResult` class. Everything remains the same. The only difference here is, instead of executing (writing) the scan request inside a method, we are writing it inside the run method.

We will write a method (see the following code block) to call the `ParallelScanner` class. First, we will create an instance of the `java.util.concurrent.ExecutorService` class with three threads. The `TotalSegments` variable decides the number of segments as well as the number of worker threads to be created for this parallel scan request. Inside the `for` loop, we instantiate the `ParallelScanner` class (created by us for parallel scanning) by calling the parameterized constructor with the parameters we will discuss later. The last two parameters are of much importance; the `totalSegments` variable has been discussed already. The variable segment is used to provide information to the `ParallelScanner` thread, to which the worker thread that does this scan result belongs.

After this, we call the execute method of the `ExecutorService` class by passing the `ParallelScanner` instance. This will invoke the run method of the `ParallelScanner` class. Since the instance is also passed while calling the execute method, this operation is thread-safe.

After initializing all the three worker threads, we will check whether the thread has finished its operation (and waiting for termination) or any exception occurred. In both the cases, we kill all the threads using the `shutdownNow` method of the `ExecutorService` class. Take a look at the following code:

```
private static void parallelScan() {
  int scanItemLimit = 100;
  int totalSegments = 3;
  ExecutorService executor = Executors
    .newFixedThreadPool(totalSegments);
  for (int segment = 0; segment < totalSegments; segment++) {
    ParallelScanner scanTask = new ParallelScanner(client,
      scanItemLimit, totalSegments, segment);
    // Execute the task
    executor.execute(scanTask);
  }
  try {
    if (!executor.awaitTermination(10, TimeUnit.SECONDS)) {
      executor.shutdownNow();
    }
  } catch (InterruptedException e) {
    executor.shutdownNow();
    Thread.currentThread().interrupt();
  }
}
```

Here, only two parameters (`segment` and `totalSegments`) will configure parallel scanning. All the other parameters are used only to configure the scan request instance (including the `scanItemLimit` variable).

Summary

In this chapter, we learned to perform simple query and scan operations on the DynamoDB table and its secondary indexes. Finally, we have also seen parallel scanning, which is good for growing and high-priority tables.

Web services and REST API are becoming more and more advanced with every passing day, mainly because of their platform-independent language. So in the next chapter, we will learn the basics of REST and how to effectively perform DynamoDB operations using REST.

6
Working with the DynamoDB API

In the previous chapter, we saw how to perform query and scan operations on DynamoDB table items using a table and its index. We also discussed parallel scanning. Most of our discussion was done using Java SDK because of the Java language's strengths. In order to perform the query and scan operations, we need to download or install certain packages onto our PC. Yet, there is a way to perform DynamoDB operations through an HTTP request. So, similar to accessing the management console, these HTTP requests to access DynamoDB are also performed through a web browser.

In this chapter, we will discuss the following topics:

- Data format
- HTTP requests
- Error handling
- Operations in DynamoDB

As part of our discussion in this chapter, we will learn about all of these topics. Before this, we should have our security credentials in hand, which we can fetch from the security page in the management console.

Data format

DynamoDB uses the **JavaScript Object Notation** (**JSON**) format to send the request to, and receive the response from, the DynamoDB endpoint. One important rule of thumb is that the DynamoDB endpoint gets this JSON request and parses it into its native format (which is not JSON). During this time, some data loss might occur because of compatibility issues. For example, JSON supports the `date` data type, but DynamoDB does not support it. So the JSON request should not have a DynamoDB incompatible data type. In order to avoid this situation, DynamoDB has already listed the allowed data types, and they are as follows:

- `S`: This denotes the `String` data type to store strings such as `"Kuppu"`
- `N`: This denotes the `Number` data type to store numbers such as 2014
- `B`: This denotes the `Binary` data type
- `SS`: This denotes the `StringSet` data type to store string sets such as `{"Uchit", "Vyas"}`
- `NS`: This denotes the `NumberSet` data type to store number sets such as `{2013, 2014}`
- `BS`: This denotes the `BinarySet` data type

Primarily, DynamoDB supports only two data types, namely, the scalar data type and multi-valued data type. S, N, and B fall under the first category, and the remaining three set types fall under the second category.

In the following example requests, all the attribute names and values will be placed within double quotes, which clearly means that all request parameters are sent as a string. So while sending binary data we need to first encode it with Base64 encoding and pass the encoded value as a string. The DynamoDB endpoint parses it by looking at whether it belongs to any of the previously mentioned data types. If it is proven negative then DynamoDB will not process this request and will send a response to the client that the JSON or request is invalid. I personally advise readers to explore the JSON syntax and its advantages, and then proceed through the rest of the chapter.

HTTP requests

As discussed in the previous section, only the request and response is in JSON format. On both the client side and the server side, this JSON data (request and response) is parsed by the SDK or the browser (on the client side) and DynamoDB (on the server side).We can perform almost all types of DynamoDB operations through HTTP requests. All the possible operations are listed, and we will discuss them in detail in the last section of this chapter. Now, let's observe the HTTP request structure. The strength of the REST API can be easily understood from the fact that most of the SDKs use REST API internally for all their calls.

Here, I have used Postman (an extension of Google Chrome) to perform the REST operations. Other than that, many other software options, such as cURL, are also available for the same purpose.

In the following screenshot, we need to understand the use of the three sections (on the right-hand side):

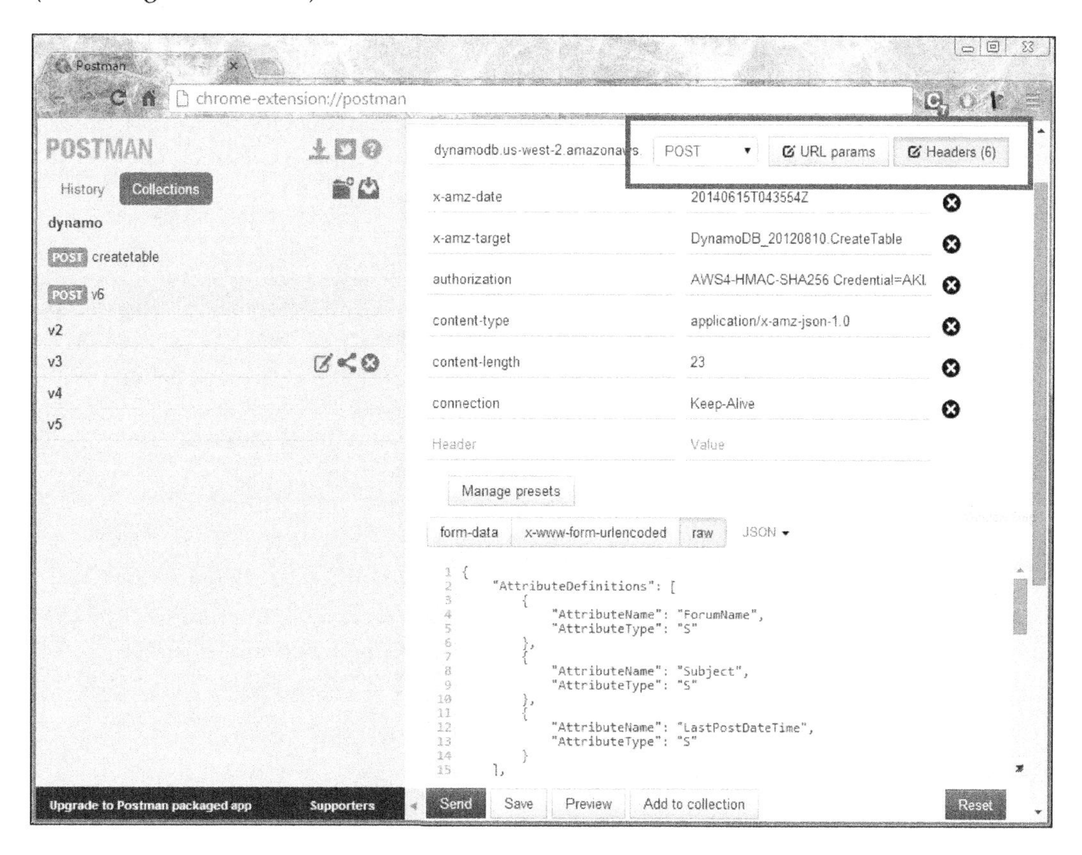

The first section has a textbox, a drop-down menu (with **POST** selected), and two buttons (**URL params** and **Headers**). This section is used to specify the information about the endpoint URL and the request method.

Clicking on the **Headers** button will open the second section, which is used to specify the header information. Here, we are adding six header elements as shown in the preceding screenshot.

The third and last section is used to provide the request body for the request. We can provide this as XML, text, or JSON. Whichever data format we choose, the body must be of the correct type. If we choose the wrong data format (or incorrect body content), the request will not reach the endpoint, and it will result in an error, which we will discuss in the next section.

Request header

The DynamoDB `POSTrequest` must have the following headers:

- `Host`: The host specifies the URL where the DynamoDB REST server (or endpoint) is located. All the requests will be redirected to this server. Our database is located at `us-west-2`, so we should specify the host as `dynamodb.us-west-2.amazonaws.com`. Instead of this, we can directly specify it in the address bar.

> As mentioned in the previous point, **Host** is also a header and every request must consist of the header **Host**. That is the reason why we don't specify it explicitly. Instead, we directly mention it in the address bar.

- `x-amz-date`: This header element is used to specify the timestamp of the request in ISO date-time format. I ran this request on June 15, 2014, at 4:35 A.M. (GMT), so I have filled it with `20140615T043554Z`.
- `x-amz-target`: This header element is used to specify what kind of DynamoDB operation has to be performed. To put it another way, this element gives a hint to the endpoint of what is written in the request body. It will usually be in the format of `DynamoDB_<API-Version>.<Table-operation>`, for example, `DynamoDB_20120810.CreateTable`.

- `authorization`: This is a complex header element. It has lots of parameters; so we will observe what is written in the previous screenshot without missing anything. The element is `AWS4-HMAC-SHA256 Credential=AKIAprabhakarK3A/20140615/us-west-2/dynamodb/aws4_request,SignedHeaders=host;x-amz-date;x-amz-target,Signature=66534aa47c45417eaac116e94abce8185cfcdea5d206981ee76a09967620ca76`. We will discuss this in detail after these bullet points.
- `content-type`: This header element is used to specify the JSON version of the request.
- `content-length`: This header element specifies the characters in the request body.
- `connection`: This header element specifies whether the request has to be kept alive even after execution, or should be terminated after some time.

Let's take a look at `AWS4-HMAC-SHA256 Credential=AKIAprabhakarK3A/20140615/us-west-2/dynamodb/aws4_request,SignedHeaders=host;x-amz-date;x-amz-target,Signature=66534aa47c45417eaac116e94abce8185cfcdea5d206981ee76a09967620ca76`. Here, the first parameter specified is the Amazon algorithm `AWS4-HMAC-SHA256`, which is used to hash the security parameters.

The second parameter is the `Credential` parameter, which is in the format access-key-ID, the current date in the `yyyy-MM-dd` format, the region where the table is available, the service name, and the termination string `aws4_request`. Each of these parameters are separated by `/`.

The third parameter, `SignedHeaders=host;x-amz-date;x-amz-target`, consists of header elements to be added to the request, with each element separated by `;`.

The last parameter, yet the most important parameter, is the `Signature` parameter (`Signature=66534aa47c45417eaac116e94abce8185cfcdea5d206981ee76a09967620ca76`). Finding or calculating this parameter is the most complex and secured. We can have a look at `http://docs.aws.amazon.com/general/latest/gr/signature-version-4.html` for further information.

Request body

All of the headers in the previous section are used for authentication and provide metadata for this REST operation. It restricts itself by saying only *how* to perform an operation; *what* to perform will be specified in the request body itself. For example, the header specifies that we need to perform table creation, but the table name, attribute configurations, and so on, must be specified in the request body.

In most of the DynamoDB operations, the request header will remain the same (except in a few places, such as `x-amz-target`, where the request header will change based on the operation we need to perform), but the request body will change for every request. So we will discuss this in the last section of this chapter.

Response header

The response header will, most probably, have six parameters. Three of those parameters (which we have already discussed) are content type, content length, and date. The other three parameters, which are new to this chapter, are listed as follows:

- `HTTP/1.1`: This header will have the status of the response to a request from the server. If it is 200, it means success, 4xx means client-side error, and 5xx means server-side error. This will be covered in detail in the next section.
- `x-amzn-RequestId`: This returned request ID can be used to debug the request.
- `x-amz-crc32`: This is the checksum returned by the DynamoDB server. We need to calculate the checksum of the returned data with this number. If the checksum doesn't match, it means somebody has done something nasty and data loss has occurred during data transfer. In this case, we must run the request once again. In the case of the SDK, this retry happens automatically.

Error handling

As discussed in the previous section, DynamoDB responds with three kinds of status codes. Response 200 means success; responses starting with 4 (400, 413, and so on) are client-side errors caused by syntax error, and responses starting with 5 (500) are server-side errors, caused because the provisioned throughput has been exceeded, the service is down, and so on.

Along with this status code, every error has an error message too. For example, a request with an invalid signature will result in a 400 error code, with the `com.amazon.coral.service#InvalidSignatureException` exception with the error message **"The request signature we calculated does not match the signature you provided. Check your AWS Secret Access Key and signing method. Consult the service documentation for details."**.

Let's see what all the possible client-side errors are. There are only two client-side status error codes. These are 400 and 413. Out of these client-side errors, a few are timing errors only. If we retry it, then it might work fine (without changing the parameters). Other errors will always fail because of a syntax error, irrespective of how many times we retry.

Client-side error with status code 400 - retry not needed

First, we will see the errors that are caused due to invalid values in the request. So, even if we retry it millions of times, it won't work.

AccessDeniedException

This is a usual authentication failure. The problem might be because of an invalid key ID or value in a request.

ConditionalCheckFailedException

This error will provide the `The conditional request failed` error message. This exception occurs when the specified (or expected) value of an attribute doesn't match the value stored in the system. An example of this case is validating an e-mail during registration to a forum. During that time, if the e-mail ID already exists in the DynamoDB table, we can throw this exception to fail the transaction.

IncompleteSignatureException

This error will be raised if one or more of the `Signature` parameters are missing. The error message shown by this error is `The request signature does not conform to AWS standards.`

LimitExceededException

This error will provide the `Too many operations for a given subscriber` error message. This exception occurs in two cases: first, because of too many simultaneous operations (more than 20 `CREATING`, `DELETING`, or `UPDATING` operations) and second, because of too many active tables (greater than 250).

MissingAuthenticationTokenException

This error will be raised if the request doesn't include the required field or the `x-amz-security-token` parameter. The error message shown by this error is `Request must contain a valid (registered) AWS Access Key ID.`

ResourceInUseException

This error will provide the `The resource which you are attempting to change is in use` error message. This exception occurs when the specified resource is already performing an operation that doesn't permit our request. An example of this case is creating a table that is already available.

ResourceNotFoundException

This error will be raised if we try to put an item on a table that is in the `CREATING` state. The error message shown by this error is `The resource which is being requested does not exist.`

ValidationException

This error will provide the `One or more required parameter values were missing` error message. This exception occurs if one or more mandatory parameters are missing.

Client-side error with status code 400 - retry possible

The client-side errors that we have seen so far will always result in errors irrespective of how many times we try (unless we debug the request). We will now see the errors that will occur only in a certain period of time. So if we retry it, it might work on the consecutive retry.

ProvisionedThroughputExceededException

This is a usual exception that occurs when too many clients are providing too many requests for a larger table simultaneously, thereby exceeding the specified throughput capacity. In the case of this error, we need to wait for a while and retry. If we use the SDK, it will take care of retrying, but in the REST request, the user has to take care of this.

ItemCollectionSizeLimitExceededException

This error will provide the `Collection size exceeded` error message. We have already come across this case in the data model and the secondary index. I will answer this case with a question. As we are already aware that a group of items that have the same hash key cannot exceed 10 GB in size, if the insertion of a new item breaks this limit, then what would happen? This exception will be thrown.

ThrottlingException

This exception will be raised if too many requests are submitted by the client rapidly and will simultaneously result in a request spike. The error message shown by this error is `Rate of requests exceeds the allowed throughput`. Since this error comes under the retry possible error with status code 400, if we retry the same operation after some time, we could get through.

UnrecognizedClientException

This error will provide the `The Access Key ID or security token is invalid` error message. This exception occurs if the access key ID or secret key is invalid.

Client-side error with status code 413

The third section of our error classification shows the error caused due to the data size limit, which in turn throws the client-side error. The only difference between the client-side errors we have seen so far and the ones we are going to see here is that the former will result in status code 400, and the latter will result in status code 413.

This error gives the `Request Entity Too Large` error message. The problem is because of the fact that the request size (or data size) has exceeded the 1 MB limit.

Server-side error with status code 500

Lastly, we will see the errors that are caused on the server side due to some issues with the server acting as the REST endpoint. For all the server-side errors, it is best practice to perform the operation again, that is, retry after some time.

InternalFailure and InternalServerError

This error will provide the `The server encountered an internal error trying to fulfill the request` error message. This exception occurs on the server side, about which the client doesn't have any information. But this error will be thrown only if the server is up and running.

ServiceUnavailableException

This exception will be raised if the service (DynamoDB, S3, and so on) is not available for use. The error message shown by this error is `The service is currently unavailable or busy`.

The sample response along with the exception message is shown in the following screenshot. In the event that an improper access key ID is provided, it will result in something similar to the following screenshot:

From the previous screenshot, a few things are clear. The status response is 400 with the `UnrecognizedClientException` exception and it took 292 ms to respond to the request. The exception class will always be mentioned in `_type`, and the corresponding error message is displayed by the key called `message`.

Error retry and exponential back off

Whenever any of the previously mentioned errors or exceptions occur, the REST client will not retry (irrespective of whether the error can be resolved by retrying) automatically. But in the case of the SDK, it will automatically retry. So it is our responsibility to program it in such a way that it retries until what we feel is the end. But there should be some reasonable delay between the retries, and this delay should increase exponentially.

Amazon recommends that we increase this delay value (starting with 50 ms) exponentially in each stage. This value can be increased until it reaches a minute. After this, we have to make this transaction fail. But it is completely in the programmer's hands. If the programmer needs to disable this retry, then he can set `maxErrorRetry` to 0.

In the case of a batch operation (`BatchGetItem` and `BatchWriteItem`), the framework will not retry the entire batch because a single batch operation can operate on multiple tables at a time. In the case of the `BatchGetItem` request, the tables and primary keys in `BatchGetItemrequests` are returned in the `UnprocessedKeys` parameter of the request. For `BatchWriteItem`, the tables and primary keys in the `BatchWriteItem` requests are returned in `UnprocessedItems`. With the help of these two parameters, we can easily retry only the failed requests.

Operations in DynamoDB

The DynamoDB REST API supports almost all the possible operations that are supported by the SDK and the management console. The possible operations are:

- `CreateTable`
- `PutItem`
- `UpdateItem`
- `GetItem`
- `Query`
- `Scan`
- `DeleteItem`
- `DescribeTable`
- `UpdateTable`
- `DeleteTable`
- `ListTables`
- `BatchGetItem`
- `BatchWriteItem`

For all of these operations, only two things will change. The first is the request body and the second is `x-amz-target`, which specifies what kind of table operation has to be performed. This attribute is the same as that of the name of the operation as shown in the previous bullet list. For example, to perform the `DescribeTable` operation, `x-amz-target` is `DynamoDB_20120810.DescribeTable` itself, so we will not be explaining it in the following text.

CreateTable

To perform the `CreateTable` operation, the request JSON will look as follows:

```
{
  "AttributeDefinitions": [
    { "AttributeName": "BookTitle", "AttributeType": "S" },
    { "AttributeName": "Author", "AttributeType": "S"},
    { "AttributeName": "PubDate","AttributeType": "S"},
    { "AttributeName": "Language", "AttributeType": "S"},
    { "AttributeName": "Edition", "AttributeType": "N" }   ],
  "TableName": "Tbl_Book",
  "KeySchema": [
    {"AttributeName": "BookTitle",  "KeyType": "HASH"},
```

```
    { "AttributeName": "Author", "KeyType": "RANGE"}    ],
  "LocalSecondaryIndexes": [
    { "IndexName": "Idx_PubDate", "KeySchema": [
      {"AttributeName": "BookTitle", "KeyType": "HASH"  },
      { "AttributeName": "PubDate","KeyType": "RANGE" }  ],
    "Projection": {  "ProjectionType": "KEYS_ONLY"   }  }  ],
  "GlobalSecondaryIndexes": [
    { "IndexName": "Idx_Pub_Edtn", "KeySchema": [
      {"AttributeName": "Language", "KeyType": "HASH"  },
      { "AttributeName": "Edition","KeyType": "RANGE" }  ],
    "Projection": {  "ProjectionType": "KEYS_ONLY"   }  }  ],
  "ProvisionedThroughput":
  {"ReadCapacityUnits": 2, "WriteCapacityUnits": 2}
}
```

The preceding code will create the `Tbl_Book` table with the same schema that we have discussed in earlier chapters. The response to this request is the same as that of the `DescribeTable` operation.

PutItem

In the previous request, we have issued a REST API command to create the table. We will now see how to insert an item into the table created by the previous request. Have a look at the following code:

```
{
  "TableName": "Tbl_Book",
  "Item": {
    "BookTitle": {"S": "SCJP" },
    "Author": {"S": "Kathy" },
    "Publisher": {"S": "TMH"},
    "PubDate": { "S": "28-Dec-09" },
    "Language": {"SS": ["English","German"] },
    "Edition" : { "N": "1"}  },
  "Expected": {
    "BookTitle": {"ComparisonOperator": "NULL", },
    "Author": {"ComparisonOperator": "NULL", }  }
}
```

The preceding code will put an item into the `Tbl_Book` table. We might question the use of a new field in the JSON called `Expected`. By default, if `SCJP` (`BookTitle`) and `Kathy` (`Author`) are already available in the table, then the older items will be replaced with the newer ones. To prevent the newer item from overwriting the older one, `ComparisonOperator` must be set to `NULL`.

UpdateItem

The following code (put in the request body) will update the item's (whose BookTitle is SCJP and Author is Kathy) Language attribute set to hold English, German, and Latin. Updating will happen only if the older value of the language set is English and German. This is the use of Expected.

```
{
  "TableName": "Tbl_Book",
  "Key": {
    "BookTitle": { "S": "SCJP"  },
    "Author": { "S": "Kathy"  }  },
  "AttributeUpdates": {
    "Language": {
      "Value": { "SS": ["English","German","Latin"]},
      "Action": "PUT"  } },
  "Expected": {
    "Language": {
      "ComparisonOperator":"EQ",
      "AttributeValueList": [ { "SS": ["English","German"]} ] }},
  "ReturnValues": "ALL_NEW"
}
```

The following code will increment the Edition attribute value of the item whose BookTitle is SCJP and Author is Kathy:

```
{
  "TableName": "Tbl_Book",
  "Key": {
    "BookTitle": { "S": "SCJP"  },
    "Author": { "S": "Kathy"  }  },
  "AttributeUpdates": {
    "Edition": {"Action": "ADD","Value": {"N": "1"}  }  },
  "ReturnValues" : "NONE"
}
```

GetItem

The following code will retrieve the BookTitle, Language, and Edition attributes of the item whose BookTitle is SCJP and Author is Kathy:

```
{
  "TableName": "Tbl_Book",
  "Key": {
    "BookTitle": { "S": "SCJP"  },
```

```
    "Author ": { "S": "Kathy" } },
  "AttributesToGet": ["BookTitle","Language","Edition"],
  "ConsistentRead": true,
  "ReturnConsumedCapacity": "TOTAL"
}
```

The preceding code will return `ConsumedCapacity`, and the result of the previous operation is as follows:

```
{
  "ConsumedCapacity": {"CapacityUnits": 1,"TableName":
    "Tbl_Book"  },
  "Item": {
    "BookTitle": { "S": "SCJP"},
    "Language": {"SS": ["English","German"]   },
    "Edition": {  "N": "1"  }}
}
```

Query

The following code will perform the query operation on index items with `PubDate` between `2009-12-28` and `2012-07-28` and `BookTitle` as `SCJP`.

```
{
  "TableName": "Tbl_Book",
  "IndexName": "Idx_PubDate",
  "Select": "ALL_ATTRIBUTES",
  "Limit":30,
  "ConsistentRead": true,
  "KeyConditions": {
    "PubDate": {
      "AttributeValueList": [{"S": "2009-12-28"},
        {"S": "2012-07-28"}],
      "ComparisonOperator": "BETWEEN"  },
    "BookTitle": {
      "AttributeValueList": [{"S": "SCJP"}],
      "ComparisonOperator": "EQ"}},
  "ReturnConsumedCapacity": "TOTAL"
}
```

Even though we have specified the item limit of the query as 30, there are only two items that satisfy these conditions. So, it returns those items, as shown in the following code:

```
{
  "Count": 2,
  "Items": [
    {
      "BookTitle": {"S": "SCJP"}, "Author": {"S": "Kathy"},
      "Publisher": {"S": "TMH"},"PubDate": {"S": "2009-12-28"},
      "Language": {"SS": ["English", "German"]}, "Edition":
        {"N": "1"}},
    {
      "BookTitle": {"S": "SCJP"}, "Author": {"S": "Khalid A M"},
      "PubDate": {"S": "2010-10-28"},"Language":
        {"SS": ["English"]}}],
  "ConsumedCapacity": {"TableName": "Tbl_Book",
    "CapacityUnits": 1}}
```

The following code returns the number of items satisfying the condition `BookTitle` equals `SCJP`:

```
{
  "TableName": "Tbl_Book",
  "Select": "COUNT",
  "ConsistentRead": true,
  "KeyConditions": {
    "BookTitle": {
      "AttributeValueList": [{"S": "SCJP"}],
      "ComparisonOperator": "EQ"}}
}
```

I think there is no need to explain what is given. It's the response to the previous request. Have a look at the following code:

```
{
  "Count":`3
}
```

Scan

The following code will scan the `Tbl_Book` table and return all the items. The response will look exactly like that of the query operation so we can skip the explanation (to save paper).

```
{
  "TableName": "Tbl_Book",
  "ReturnConsumedCapacity": "TOTAL"
}
```

The following code will apply a scan filter (`Publisher` must be `TMH`) to the scan operation:

```
{
  "TableName": "Tbl_Book",
  "ScanFilter": {
    "Publisher": {
      "AttributeValueList": [{"S": "TMH"}],
      "ComparisonOperator": "EQ"}},
  "ReturnConsumedCapacity": "TOTAL"
}
```

DeleteItem

The following code will delete the item whose `BookTitle` is `SCJP` and `Author` is `Kathy`. The response to this request will display the deleted item's attributes and values.

```
{
  "TableName": "Tbl_Book",
  "Key": {"BookTitle": { "S": "SCJP" },"Author":
    { "S": "Kathy"  }  },
  "ReturnValues": "ALL_OLD"
}
```

DescribeTable

The following code will display all the table schema of the table with the name `Tbl_Book`. As hinted in the `CreateTable` command, the response of the `DescribeTable` and `CreateTable` requests will be similar (except `TableStatus`). After performing the `CreateTable` request, `TableStatus` will be `CREATING`. So if we describe the same table after a point of time (once the table has become active), its status will become `ACTIVE`.

Have a look at the following code:

```
{
  "TableName":"Tbl_Book"
}
```

The following is the output of `DescribeTable` with `TableStatus` as `ACTIVE`:

```
{
  "Table": {
    "AttributeDefinitions": [
      { "AttributeName": "BookTitle", "AttributeType": "S" },
      { "AttributeName": "Author", "AttributeType": "S"},
      { "AttributeName": "PubDate","AttributeType": "S"},
      { "AttributeName": "Language", "AttributeType": "S"},
      { "AttributeName": "Edition", "AttributeType": "N" }   ],
    "CreationDateTime": 1.363729002358E9,
    "ItemCount": 5,
    "KeySchema": [
      {"AttributeName": "BookTitle","KeyType": "HASH"},
      {"AttributeName": "Author","KeyType": "RANGE"}],
    "LocalSecondaryIndexes": [
      { "IndexName": "Idx_PubDate", "KeySchema": [
        {"AttributeName": "BookTitle", "KeyType": "HASH"  },
        { "AttributeName": "PubDate","KeyType": "RANGE" }  ],
      "Projection": {  "ProjectionType": "KEYS_ONLY"  }  }  ],
    "GlobalSecondaryIndexes": [
      { "IndexName": "Idx_Pub_Edtn", "KeySchema": [
        {"AttributeName": "Language", "KeyType": "HASH"  },
        { "AttributeName": "Edition","KeyType": "RANGE" }  ],
      "Projection": {  "ProjectionType": "KEYS_ONLY"  }  }  ],
    "ProvisionedThroughput": {
      "NumberOfDecreasesToday":0,
      "ReadCapacityUnits":5,"WriteCapacityUnits":5},
    "TableName": "Tbl_Book","TableSizeBytes": 0,
    "TableStatus": "ACTIVE" }
}
```

UpdateTable

The following request will update the table's provisioned throughput capacity (both read and write) to `5`:

```
{
  "TableName": "Tbl_Book",
  "ProvisionedThroughput": {"ReadCapacityUnits":5,
    "WriteCapacityUnits":5}
}
```

DeleteTable

One of the simplest DynamoDB REST API requests is to delete a table. To delete a table named `Tbl_Book`, the request body should have the following JSON:

```
{
  "TableName": "Tbl_Book"
}
```

The following is the response to the `DeleteTable` request, displaying information about the table being deleted:

```
{
  "TableDescription": {
    "ItemCount": 5,
    "ProvisionedThroughput": {
      "NumberOfDecreasesToday": 0,
      "ReadCapacityUnits": 5,"WriteCapacityUnits": 5},
    "TableName": "Tbl_Book","TableSizeBytes": 0,
    "TableStatus": "DELETING"}
}
```

ListTables

The following code lists not more than three tables whose names begin with or alphabetically come after `Tbl_Book`. For example, if we have three tables in our DynamoDB, namely, `Tbl_Book`, `Tbl_Library`, and `Table_One`, the following request will return only `Tbl_Book` and `Tbl_Library`. The reason why `Table_One` will not be returned is that if we sort the three tables based on alphabetical order of their names, `Table_One` will take first place, `Tbl_Book` will take second place, and `Tbl_Library` will take third place. Here we are performing the list operation with `ExclusiveStartTableName` as `Tbl_Book`.

Because of the fact that alphabetically `Table_One` comes prior to `Tbl_Book`, it is not returned.

```
{
  "ExclusiveStartTableName": "Tbl_Book","Limit": 3
}
```

We have only two tables in our account. So, the response will have only two table names in the array, as follows:

```
{
  "LastEvaluatedTableName": "Tbl_Library",
  "TableNames": ["Tbl_Book","Tbl_Library"]
}
```

BatchGetItem

If we need to read data from multiple tables at the same time, then the `BatchGetItem` operation is advised. It is advised to use this operation whenever and wherever possible because it consumes the read throughput equally across all the tables in question. The following code tries to fetch three items from `Tbl_Library` and one item from `Tbl_Book`:

```
{
  "RequestItems": {
    "Tbl_Library": {
      "Keys": [
        {"Name":{"S":"Library of Congress"}},
        {"Name":{"S":"National Diet Library"}},
        {"Name":{"S":"Royal Danish Library"}}],
      "AttributesToGet": ["Country","City"]},
    "Tbl_Book": {
      "Keys": [
        {"BookTitle": { "S": "SCJP" }, "Author ":
          { "S": "Kathy" } }],
      "AttributesToGet": ["BookTitle","Language","Edition"]}},
  "ReturnConsumedCapacity": "TOTAL"
}
```

The response of the `BatchGetItem` operation is as follows:

```
{
  "Responses": {
    "Tbl_Library": [
      {
        "Name":{"S":"Library of Congress"},
```

```
          "Country":{"S":"United States"},
            "City":{"S":"WashingtonDC"} },
        {
          "Name":{"S":"National Diet Library"},
          "Country":{"S":"Japan"},"City":{"S":"Tokyo"} },
        {
          "Name":{"S":"Royal Danish Library"},
          "Country":{"S":"Denmark"},"City":{"S":"Copenhagen"} }]
      "Tbl_Book": [
        {
          "BookTitle": { "S": "SCJP" },
          "Language": { "SS": ["English","German"]    },
          "Edition": {   "N": "1"    } }]},
    "UnprocessedKeys": {},
    "ConsumedCapacity": [
      {"TableName": "Tbl_Library","CapacityUnits": 3},
      {"TableName": "Tbl_Book","CapacityUnits": 1}]
  }
```

BatchWriteItem

If we need to write data to multiple tables at the same time, then the `BatchWriteItem` operation is advised whenever and wherever possible, because it distributes the write throughput equally across all the tables. The following request tries to write two items into `Tbl_Library` and one item into `Tbl_Book`. It is also possible to send `DeleteRequest` in place of `PutRequest` simultaneously for a table. Have a look at the following table:

```
  {
    "RequestItems": {
      "Tbl_Library": [
        {
          "PutRequest": {
            "Item": {
              "Name":{"S":"Harvard University Library"},
              "Country":{"S":"United States"},
              "City":{"S":"Massachusetts"} } } },
        {
          "PutRequest": {
            "Item": {
              "Name":{"S":"Vernadsky National Library"},
              "Country":{"S":"Ukraine"},
              "City":{"S":"Kiev"} } } }]
      "Tbl_Book": [
```

```
        {
          "PutRequest": {
            "Item": {
              "BookTitle": { "S": "SCJP" },
              "Author": { "S": "Brendon" },
              "Language":{ "SS": ["English"] },
              "Edition": {  "N": "5" } }} } ]},
    "ReturnConsumedCapacity": "TOTAL"
  }
```

The response to the previous `BatchWriteItem` request is shown as follows:

```
  {
    "UnprocessedItems": { },
    "ConsumedCapacity": [
      {"TableName": "Tbl_Library","CapacityUnits": 2},
      {"TableName": "Tbl_Book","CapacityUnits": 1}]
  }
```

Summary

In this chapter, we have learned how to use the REST API to perform DynamoDB operations. We have also learned about a few things that we never came across in previous chapters (take `BatchWriteItem` and `BatchGetItem` for instance). The usage of batch operations will provide the output in a faster way, because all table data is queried or written in parallel. One tradeoff is that it consumes a lot of capacity units. In simple words, using the batch operation will give you an optimized result, but you might have to pay more.

In the next chapter, we will learn about the distributed locking used in DynamoDB for transaction management. In the case of multitenant systems, this locking mechanism is pretty important because of batch operations and because multiple users might write or read data simultaneously. Without implementing locking techniques in our application, we will always get unacceptable responses and the application will nosedive. We will also see the Java high-level API for DynamoDB interaction.

7
Distributed Locking with DynamoDB

In the previous chapter, we saw how to perform all the DynamoDB operations using the REST API. We also discussed in detail each and every JSON request used and its response, and understood that even a simple browser is more powerful in the hands of an intelligent programmer. DynamoDB is a distributed and redundant database, which means two things. The first thing is that every large set of table data will be distributed among multiple servers, and the second thing is that every item (copy of the data) will be made available on multiple servers so that even if one server becomes unresponsive, we can still read it from other servers. Even though both are good for us, there are a few tradeoffs. One of the most critical tradeoffs in almost all distributed (and redundant) databases is data synchronization across all the redundant servers. So, in this chapter, we will see how distributed locking helps DynamoDB to manage data synchronization and redundancy.

In this chapter, we will discuss the following topics:

- Distributed locking
- Java high-level API
- Optimistic locking
- Importance of distributed locking

As a part of our discussion in this chapter, we will learn about all of these topics. Before we begin, we should have some knowledge of the DynamoDB high-level API, which we will discuss in a while.

Distributed locking

To demonstrate the idea of distributed locking, let us relate it to something that programmers use commonly to share it among your project team. Consider **Team Foundation Server** (**TFS**) or SVN (Apache Subversion), which we commonly use to manage the team's program code. If you don't get what we are talking about, please refer to `http://en.wikipedia.org/wiki/Apache_Subversion`. In both these pieces of software, any number of permitted team members can read a code and download the latest code to his/her local machine and start editing. After editing the program, one programmer synchronizes his/her program with the SVN repository. What this means is that all other programmers are making changes to the obsolete program. So, if any other programmer tries to commit his/her code, SVN issues a warning and will not permit the user to do so.

As far as DynamoDB is concerned, why do we need distributed locking? It's because, once we start using the DynamoDB table, everything is fine. Apart from us, no one is going to access it. But, consider an application backed up by DynamoDB. Are we sure that only one user will use the application and perform write operations at one time? We cannot predict that. This is the reason why we need to lock data just in case the same data is accessed by another client at the same time. DynamoDB provides this distributed locking through a mechanism called optimistic locking, which we will discuss at the end of this chapter. First, let us observe a real-time example where locking is important.

Let's take a look at some real-life examples. Let's wind the clocks back a decade or a couple of years. Imagine that we are back at school and having a look at the following color mixer:

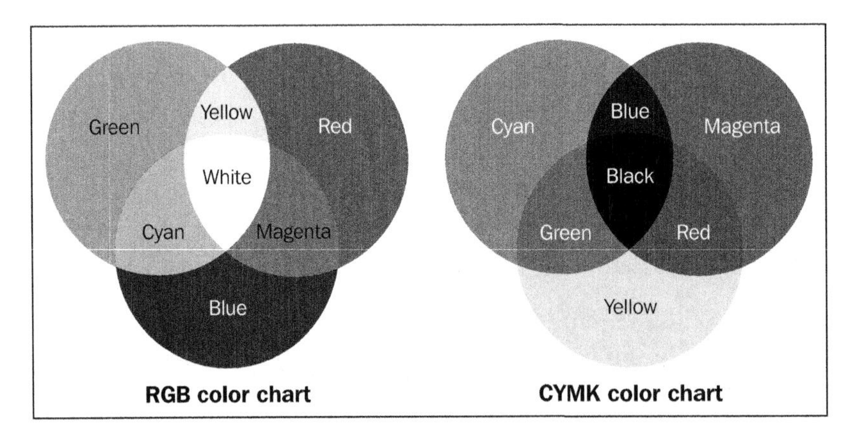

The **RGB color chart** says that if we mix the green and blue color paint or dye, we will get the color cyan, and we can mix two colors as shown in the preceding diagram to get the necessary color. There is a family with three members, and each member is given one of the primary colors (red, blue, and green). They are asked to prepare the white paint to paint their living room. The mixing room is very small, and only one person can enter at a time. Now anyone can enter the room in any order. After all of them mix the colors red, blue and green in the correct proportion, the family will get the white paint. We don't have any problem in this case.

Consider another scenario where we need black paint. As mentioned in the **CMYK color chart**, if we need black then we must mix cyan, magenta, and yellow in equal proportions. Therefore now we have two mixing rooms. The first mixing room is used to produce the colors cyan, magenta, and yellow, and the second mixer room is used to mix these colors to get the color black. Therefore, the first mixing room should have three containers. Each family member holding a primary color (red, green, and blue) should mix their color in exactly two containers. For example, to get cyan, we need to mix blue and green. If the person holding red mixes his color with the container that always has cyan, then it will turn white, which makes the whole process fail. So there should be some locking, which is made available.

Let us assume that the father and mother have the colors red and blue with them and have done their work by mixing the paints in the correct containers. So, as of now, one container will have magenta (R+B), the other will have red, and the last container will have blue. Then their elder son enters with green paint and mixes it in the second container, which turns into yellow (R+G). He then realizes that he doesn't have any paint left to mix with the third container which is still blue. So, he moves out to collect the paint. The younger daughter doesn't have any idea about it. So, she comes and collects all three containers and mixes them. Do you think she might have looked at the color black? The answer is no, and in fact, she will look at magenta. Y+M gives red and R+B gives magenta.

The question is, what might have prevented this error? First, it is the responsibility of the elder son to notify the family members that he is not yet done with his work and he should have put a lock on that room, not letting anyone (including his sister) mix those paints prematurely. But, he didn't do that. This is the reason why we should have a lock over something (here the DynamoDB database table) when more than one person has access to the shared data. Even though it is a bigger illustration, I hope that it answers the primary question about the use of locking.

The preceding image is available as a colored image for download from `https://www.packtpub.com/sites/default/files/downloads/1897OT_07_01.png`.

Solutions available to solve distributed writes

DynamoDB already has two solutions (so far) to synchronize the writes of multiple users or clients. Let us list those solutions:

- Adding the client requests to **Simple Queue Service** (**SQS**)
- Using of conditional writes (as discussed in the *Operations in DynamoDB* section in *Chapter 6, Working with the DynamoDB API*)

SQS allows us to store messages in a highly reliable, scalable queue, which is hosted by AWS as a service. In a distributed and scalable environment, all the messages from applications might not directly be destined to be stored in a database. In order to set the destination for these messages, they need to be added to a reliable queue such as SQS.

The first solution is a little advanced, because it requires knowledge of Amazon SQS. In this, all the DynamoDB requests will be redirected to SQS. There is an internal mechanism in SQS that will not allow multiple readers on the same data. Because of this, until the first client is done with his work, no one else can read the data. This way, we can avoid concurrent writing of data.

Let us see the syntax of the `UpdateItem` request, otherwise we might not be sailing in the same boat:

```
{
  "TableName": "Tbl_Book",
  "Key": {
    "BookTitle": { "S": "SCJP"  },
    "Author": { "S": "Kathy"   }  },
  "AttributeUpdates": {
    "Language": {
      "Value": { "SS": ["English","German","Latin"]},
      "Action": "PUT"   } },
  "ReturnValues": "ALL_NEW"
}
```

The preceding update operation was performed on the table with `["English","German"]` as the content of the `Language` set.

The REST request body will update the item that has `BookTitle` as `SCJP` and `Author` as `Kathy`, thereby updating the `Language` set to hold English, German, and Latin. Now, let's say that the same book has been published in another language (Greek). So, another update request comes in from another client (who doesn't know that Latin is also there in the `Language` set), as shown in the following code:

```
{
  "TableName": "Tbl_Book",
  "Key": {
    "BookTitle": { "S": "SCJP"  },
    "Author": { "S": "Kathy"  }  },
  "AttributeUpdates": {
    "Language": {
      "Value": { "SS": ["English","German","Greek"]},
      "Action": "PUT"  } },
  "ReturnValues": "ALL_NEW"
}
```

Now, what happened? Even though the SCJP book written by Kathy is available in Latin, it won't be available. So, what might have prevented this error is the use of the `Expected` field in the request. This is because, before adding a value to a `Language` set, the user should have checked whether his/her update operation will affect or overwrite any useful information that is already available in the set.

It is time to take a look at the code to avoid this issue. The code using the `Expected` field in the `UpdateItem` request body is as follows:

```
{
  "TableName": "Tbl_Book",
  "Key": {
    "BookTitle": { "S": "SCJP"  },
    "Author": { "S": "Kathy"  }  },
  "AttributeUpdates": {
    "Language": {
      "Value": { "SS": ["English","German","Greek"]},
      "Action": "PUT"  } },
  "Expected": {
    "Language": {
      "ComparisonOperator":"EQ",
      "AttributeValueList":
      [ { "SS": ["English","German"] } ]  } },
  "ReturnValues": "ALL_NEW"
}
```

The highlighted lines will perform this control. The second user, before placing the `UpdateItem` request to add Greek to the `Language` set, is checking whether the current content of the `Language` set is `["English","German"]`. Here, this condition will fail because of the first `UpdateItem` request executed by the first user, due to which the `Language` set will have `["English","German","Latin"]`. So now the second user will change his/her query as shown in the following code, which will add the new language to the set without any trouble:

```
{
  "TableName": "Tbl_Book",
  "Key": {
    "BookTitle": { "S": "SCJP"  },
    "Author": { "S": "Kathy"  }  },
  "AttributeUpdates": {
    "Language": {
      "Value": { "SS":
        ["English","German","Latin","Greek"]},
      "Action": "PUT"  } },
  "Expected": {
    "Language": {
      "ComparisonOperator":"EQ",
      "AttributeValueList":
      [ { "SS": ["English","German","Latin"] } ] } },
  "ReturnValues": "ALL_NEW"
}
```

A similar kind of explanation of how to avoid distributed writes in DynamoDB is given in detail at `http://docs.aws.amazon.com/amazondynamodb/latest/developerguide/WorkingWithItems.html#WorkingWithItems.ConditionalUpdate`. There really is a pretty good illustration given in the link.

The use of `Expectedfield` is not just restricted to REST API. The same is possible in the Java low-level API too (which we have discussed in *Chapter 3, Tools and Libraries of AWS DynamoDB*). Even though the preceding code snippets seem simple, both of these methods indirectly lock the write on the table items. In some cases these might fail.

Let's discuss a locking mechanism available with DynamoDB called optimistic locking. This technique is not available in the Java low-level API we have used so far. This technique is only available in the Java high-level API. So, let's learn the Java high-level API first, and then we will move our focus to optimistic locking.

Java high-level API

For those who have an idea about **Java Database Connectivity** (**JDBC**) and **Java Persistence API** (**JPA**), DynamoDB's Java low-level API is like JDBC and DynamoDB's Java high-level API is like JPA, which allows us to map a DynamoDB table with a Java class. Therefore, setting the values to the instance variable is like adding attributes to the item. This is what we call **object-relational mapping** (**ORM**). But in DynamoDB, we call this by a different name, and that is object persistence model.

In a high-level API, a Java class is directly mapped to a DynamoDB table, because of which a large amount of redundant code and conditions can be avoided. Another advantage with this API is that it comes with a few methods, such as save, load, and delete, which are thread safe and allow us to enact locking techniques.

Now, let's create a class to be mapped to the `Tbl_Book` table in DynamoDB.

```
@DynamoDBTable(tableName="Tbl_Book")
public class BookEntity {
  private String BookTitle;
  private String Author;
  private String PubDate;
  private String Publisher;
  private Integer Edition;
  private Set<String> Language;
  @DynamoDBHashKey(attributeName="BookTitle")
  public String getBookTitle() {
    return BookTitle;
  }
  public void setBookTitle(String bookTitle) {
    BookTitle = bookTitle;
  }
  @DynamoDBAttribute(attributeName="Author")
  public String getAuthor() {
    return Author;
  }
  public void setAuthor(String author) {
    Author = author;
  }
  @DynamoDBRangeKey(attributeName="PubDate")
  public String getPubDate() {
    return PubDate;
  }
  public void setPubDate(String pubDate) {
    PubDate = pubDate;
  }
```

```
    @DynamoDBAttribute(attributeName="Publisher")
    public String getPublisher() {
      return Publisher;
    }
    public void setPublisher(String publisher) {
      Publisher = publisher;
    }
    @DynamoDBAttribute(attributeName="Edition")
    public Integer getEdition() {
      return Edition;
    }
    public void setEdition(Integer edition) {
      Edition = edition;
    }
    @DynamoDBAttribute(attributeName="Language")
    public Set<String>getLanguage() {
      return Language;
    }
    public void setLanguage(Set<String> language) {
      Language = language;
    }

  }
```

The `@DynamoDBTable(tableName="Tbl_Book")` annotation will map the `BookEntity` class to the DynamoDB `Tbl_Book` table. The hash-type attribute's (`BookTitle`) getter (`getBookTitle`) will be followed by the `@DynamoDBHashKey(attributeName="BookTitle")` annotation and the range attribute's getter (`getAuthor`) will be followed by the `@DynamoDBRangeKey(attributeName="Author")` annotation.

All other attributes (`BookTitle`, `Author`, `PubDate`, `Publisher`, `Edition`, and `Language`) getters will be followed by the `@DynamoDBAttribute(attributeName="")` annotation with the corresponding table attribute name. We have seen how to represent primary key and non-key attributes. Now, let's see how an item can be put on the DynamoDB table using a high-level API. Take a look at the following code:

```
AmazonDynamoDBClient dynamoDBClient = new AmazonDynamoDBClient(
  new ProfileCredentialsProvider());
DynamoDBMapper dynamoDBMapper = new
  DynamoDBMapper(dynamoDBClient);
  BookEntity book = new BookEntity();
  book.setBookTitle("Hadoop");
  book.setAuthor("Tom White");
  book.setEdition(new Integer(1));
```

```
book.setPubDate("2012-12-28");
book.setPublisher("o'reilly");
book.setLanguage(new
  HashSet<String>(Arrays.asList("English")));
dynamoDBMapper.save(book);
```

The preceding code will put an item with the given details. The first line of the code creates a client for DynamoDB and the second line will create a `DynamoDBMapper` class for this client. Then, the next seven lines will create an instance of the `BookEntity` class (mapped to the `Tbl_Book` table) and populate it with the corresponding data. Then, the last line will call the save method available in the `DynamoDBMapper` class, which will put this item in the table. Let's see how we can perform a query operation using the high-level API:

```
BookEntity bookEntity = new BookEntity();
bookEntity.setBookTitle("Hadoop");
bookEntity.setPubDate("2012-12-28");
DynamoDBQueryExpression<BookEntity> query
  = new DynamoDBQueryExpression<BookEntity>()
    .withHashKeyValues(bookEntity);
query.setHashKeyValues(bookEntity);
List<BookEntity> bookList
  = dynamoDBMapper.query(BookEntity.class, query);
for (BookEntity book : bookList) {
  System.out.println
    (book.getBookTitle()+"\t"+book.getEdition()
      + "\t" + book.getLanguage());
}
```

The high-level API is a very vast topic to discuss. But for our discussion about optimistic locking, this much knowledge is enough.

Optimistic locking

Optimistic locking is a strategy by which all the write requests (put, update, or delete) will succeed only after ensuring that the client (performing the write request) and the server have the same data version. If anyone else updates this data (which will change the data version) then the client cannot perform this write operation. We will look at optimistic locking in detail. Let's just add an attribute to the `BookEntity` class we saw previously:

```
@DynamoDBTable(tableName="Tbl_Book")
publicclassBookEntity {
  private Longversion;
  ...
```

```
    @DynamoDBVersionAttribute
    public LonggetVersion() {
      returnversion;
    }
    publicvoidsetVersion(Longversion) {
      this.version = version;
    }
}
```

The preceding class is not complete and shows only the new fields. For the complete structure, merge this with the older BookEntity class we saw previously.

We are adding an attribute to control the version-based locking named version. Then, we create getters and setters, and then the getter of version is made to have a @DynamoDBVersionAttribute annotation. These are the changes to be made in the BookEntity class.

Once we are done with this, then every write operation (save and delete) performed on BookEntity using the DynamoDBMapper class will check whether the client and the server have the same version attribute. When a new item is put into the table, the value of the version attribute will be 1. For further update operation, this value will be incremented by 1. Therefore, let us assume that our code retrieved the freshly put item from Tbl_Book with the values discussed in the *Java high-level API* section. Since this is a newly put item, the version attribute will have the value 1.

Now let's say that a program (a general one) reads this item in line 20 (we are not talking about any program written here. The line number used is only for illustration purposes), creates another table named Tbl_Library, and waits until the table becomes active. Meanwhile another client has updated the Language attribute of the item from ["English"] to ["English","German"]. So this operation will increment the version attribute.

Now let's say that in line 40 (we are not talking about any program written here; the line number used here is only for illustration purposes), we are trying to delete the read item. What will happen? It will not delete the item. The reason is simple: now the server will have the version attribute (of this item) as 2 (because of the update operation, which incremented the version value), and the client will have the version attribute value as 1 (because it doesn't know that an update operation has been performed on the item). Because of the mismatch with the server-side and the client-side version attribute values, this operation will fail. This is called optimistic locking. Optimistic locking will happen automatically (provided the class has an attribute with the @DynamoDBVersionAttribute annotation) and it is enabled by default.

> If an instance variable of the mapped class (`BookTitle`) has `@DynamoDBVersionAttribute`, this attribute will also be inserted into the table along with the other attributes of the item. Therefore, the size of the item will become bigger. So, the version attribute name must be as small as possible.

Try to run the following code to check whether it is gives any error:

```
try {
  BookEntity book = dynamoDBMapper.load(
    BookEntity.class, "Hadoop","2012-12-28");
  if(book!=null)
    System.out.println(book.getBookTitle()
    + "\t" + book.getEdition() + "\t" + book.getLanguage());
  book.setLanguage(new HashSet<String>(Arrays.asList
    ("English", "German")));
  dynamoDBMapper.save(book);

  BookEntity book1 = dynamoDBMapper.load(
    BookEntity.class, "Hadoop","2012-12-28");
  if(book!=null)
    System.out.println(book.getBookTitle() + "\t" +
      book.getEdition()
      + "\t" + book.getLanguage());
  book1.setLanguage(new HashSet<String>(
    Arrays.asList("English", "German", "Latin")));
  dynamoDBMapper.save(book1);
} catch (ConditionalCheckFailedException e) {
  System.out.println(e.getMessage());
}
```

Running the preceding code will not give any error because we get the `BookEntity` item using the key values `Hadoop` and `2012-12-28`. Then, we set the `Language` set to hold English and German strings to the returned `BookEntity` item and save it (which ends the first transaction and updates the version attribute). The code will print the following output:

```
Hadoop 1 [Latin, German, English]
Hadoop 1 [German, English]
```

Running the following code will result in `ConditionalCheckFailedException`. It is exactly the same as that of the previous code, except for the location of `dynamoDBMapper.save(book)`:

```
try {
  BookEntity book = dynamoDBMapper.load(
    BookEntity.class, "Hadoop","2012-12-28");
  if(book!=null)
    System.out.println(book.getBookTitle()
      + "\t" + book.getEdition() + "\t" + book.getLanguage());
  book.setLanguage(new HashSet<String>
    (Arrays.asList("English", "German")));

  BookEntity book1 = dynamoDBMapper.load(
    BookEntity.class, "Hadoop","2012-12-28");
  if(book!=null)
    System.out.println(book.getBookTitle() + "\t" +
      book.getEdition()
      + "\t" + book.getLanguage());
  book1.setLanguage(new HashSet<String>(
    Arrays.asList("English", "German", "Latin")));
  dynamoDBMapper.save(book1);
  dynamoDBMapper.save(book);
} catch (ConditionalCheckFailedException e) {
  System.out.println(e.getMessage());
}
```

It will print the following error message:

```
The conditional request failed (Service: AmazonDynamoDBv2; Status
  Code: 400; Error Code: ConditionalCheckFailedException;
```

In the previous code block, what we do is this: first, we retrieve `BookEntity` with the key values `Hadoop` and `2012-12-28`, which will fetch the version attribute (let's say that the value is `1`). Then, after printing the entity parameters, we update the item by setting the `Language` set to `"English", "German"`.

Second, we again retrieve `BookEntity` with the key values `Hadoop` and `2012-12-28`, which will fetch the version attribute too (the value will remain `1`, because no write operation has been performed yet on the item). Again, we print the entity parameters, and then we update the item by setting the `Language` set to `"English"`, `"German"`, `"Latin"`. Then we try to save the second retrieved item. This item will be saved (or updated) without any error, because the version attribute value still remains `1`. This update operation will increment the version attribute value by `1`. So, its value changes to `2`, so in the next line, we save the first updated item. This will throw the `ConditionalCheckFailedException` exception, because during the retrieval of the item, the version attribute value was `1`, but now (due to the last update operation) its value has become `2`. This clearly means that `DynamoDBMapper` is trying to write an obsolete item, which is no longer allowed.

If we want to disable this optimistic locking, we can rewrite our block with the following code:

```
dynamoDBMapper.save(book1, new DynamoDBMapperConfig(
  DynamoDBMapperConfig.SaveBehavior.CLOBBER));
dynamoDBMapper.save(book, new DynamoDBMapperConfig(
  DynamoDBMapperConfig.SaveBehavior.CLOBBER));
```

This will enforce overwriting values irrespective of whether the data is obsolete or not.

Importance of distributed locking

Locking is one of the most important synchronization techniques in a database. It is a must if multiple users are interacting with it simultaneously. The use of a high-level API (along with a version attribute in the mapping class) ensures locking. In the case of a multiuser, multiserver database environment, if distributed locking is not incorporated then most of the users may well be sitting on the detached branch of the tree and working on obsolete data. The importance is actually in deciding whether we need this locking, because as a tradeoff every item will have an attribute especially to manage versions or locking, which might itself eat up a lot of space and throughput capacity.

Summary

We began the chapter by discussing the need to lock in a distributed environment. Then, we started learning the Java high-level API, which is mandatory to start with distributed locking since it is not available with low-level APIs. Then, we learned the meaning of distributed locking and its usage. We also discussed how distributed locking can be realized using optimistic locking.

Every Amazon web service has its own advantages. So in the next chapter, we will learn about integrating DynamoDB with Redshift, Data Pipeline, and MapReduce.

8

DynamoDB with Redshift, Data Pipeline, and MapReduce

In the previous chapter, we learned the meaning of distributed locking and its usage. We have also gone through how distributed locking can be realized using optimistic locking. Until now, we were learning deep insights into DynamoDB's technical aspects and its configurations. So, in this chapter, we will be able to learn how to use DynamoDB with other AWS services and how to integrate it with the computational and analyzing services of AWS. We will learn to perform the following actions:

- Loading data from DynamoDB into Redshift
- Transferring data between DynamoDB and S3
- Exporting, importing, querying, and joining tables using AWS MapReduce

As we go through the discussion in this chapter, we will learn about all of these topics. So let's start the journey with the first topic, which will be a combination of DynamoDB and Redshift.

Loading data from DynamoDB into Redshift

Amazon Redshift will give great results by integrating with Amazon DynamoDB. Integration of both services will give you advanced business intelligence capabilities and a powerful SQL-based interface for database administrators and developers. By copying data from an Amazon DynamoDB table to Amazon Redshift clustered instances, you can perform any complex data analysis queries on the given data, including all joins. You can transfer all of your Amazon DynamoDB data from tables into an Amazon Redshift table using just a single command run from within Amazon Redshift. To load data into Redshift from DynamoDB, you have to first create tables in Redshift. The table can be temporary or persistent. The `COPY` command will affix new inputs as data to any existing rows in the table:

```
copytable_uchitredshift from 'dynamodb:// table_uchitdynamodb'
credentials 'aws_access_key_id=xxxxx;aws_secret_access_key=xxx'
readratio 50;
```

In this example, the source table in DynamoDB is `table_uchitdynamodb`. The target table in Amazon Redshift is `table_uchitredshift`. The `readratio 50` clause regulates the percentage of provisioned throughput that is consumed. In this case, the `COPY` command will use only 50 percent of the read capacity units provisioned for `table_uchitdynamodb`. I recommend setting the ratio to a value less than the average unused provisioned throughput because a lower value will minimize throttling issues.

For the `COPY` command, you must have the `INSERT` privilege on the Amazon Redshift table.

Remember that you are transferring data from a NoSQL environment to a SQL environment; so there are certain rules in one environment that won't work in another environment. The rules can be as follows:

- The DynamoDB table names are case sensitive, whereas in Amazon Redshift they are not.
- The DynamoDB table names can contain up to 255 characters, including "." (dot) and "-" (dash), whereas in Amazon Redshift table names are limited to 127 characters. Also, in DynamoDB, you are allowed ASCII letters, digits, underscore characters (_), or dollar signs ($) for standard SQL identifiers.
- Amazon Redshift-reserved keywords cannot be used as table names.

- DynamoDB does not support the null concept of SQL.
- DynamoDB data types do not match completely with those of Amazon Redshift.

Throughput will count against that table's read capacity. So, once you are done with the copying process, your queries written in Redshift won't be affected in any manner in DynamoDB.

> The DynamoDB data must be created in the same region as your cluster, otherwise, you have to explicitly mention the region in which your actual DynamoDB table has been created. This can also be done using the `REGION` parameter.

Using the `COPY` command, Amazon Redshift can leverage the **massively parallel processing (MPP)** architecture to load and read data from the DynamoDB table. The `COPY` command will match the attribute names with the data retrieved from the DynamoDB table, to column names with the existing Redshift table, by the previously mentioned rules.

Importing and exporting data between DynamoDB and S3

To start transferring between DynamoDB and S3 using AWS Data Pipeline, there are some prerequisites that you have to fulfill first. They are as follows:

1. Be familiar with the AWS Data Pipeline console. The following is the console screenshot, and its overview has been added so that you can go through it:

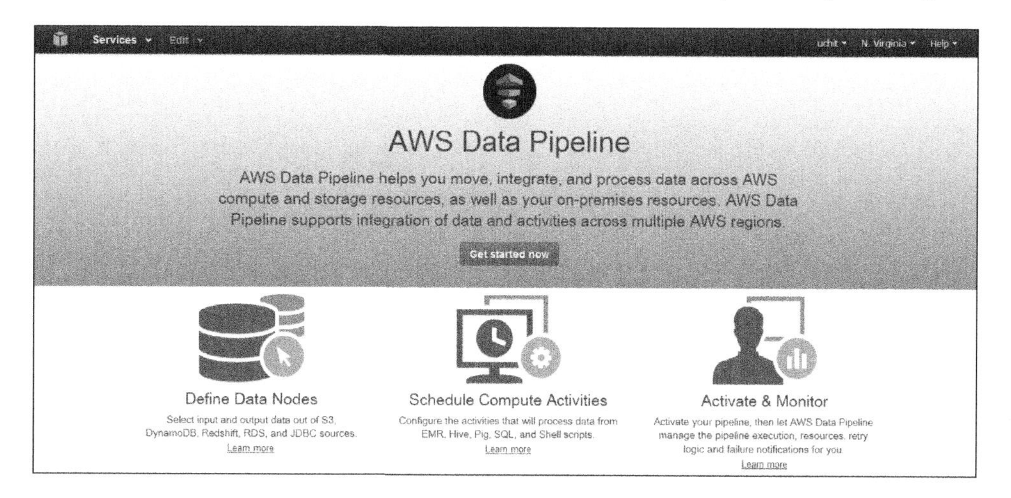

2. The first page you see will be the previous screenshot. By clicking on **Get started now**, you will be redirected to the following page to configure your AWS Data Pipeline:

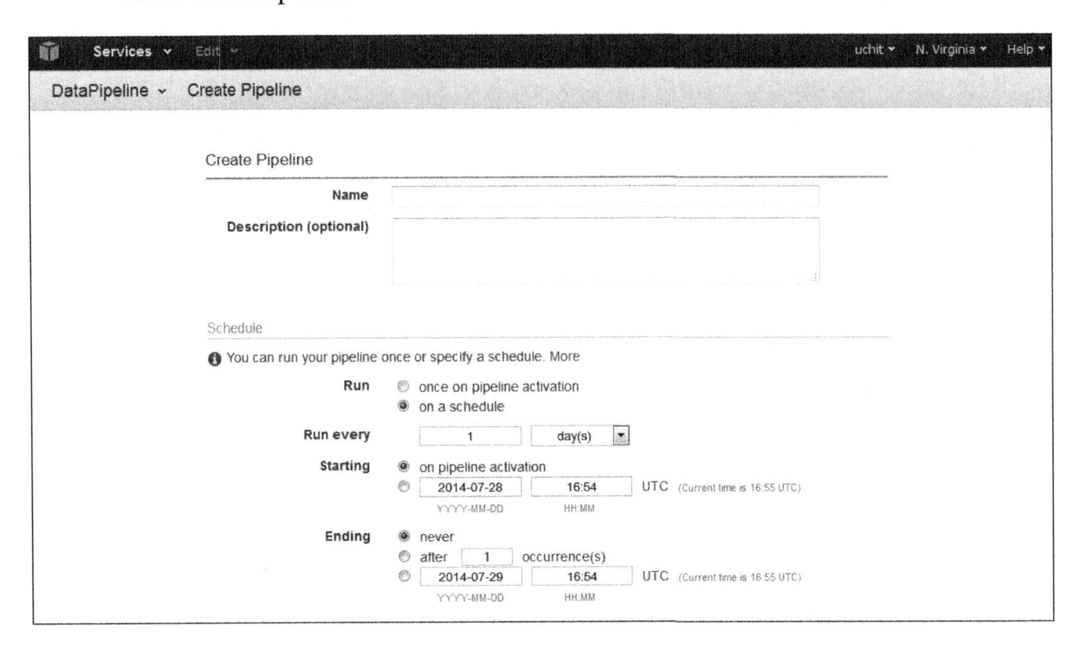

Now, by providing details for the given fields you can set up the Data Pipeline service. Create the following objects:

1. The S3 bucket as the source for your data.
2. A DynamoDB table.
3. An SNS topic. Subscribe to it to receive notifications from AWS Data Pipeline regarding the status of your pipeline components.

Before transferring data between DynamoDB and S3, there are couples of points that you need to keep in mind. They are as follows:

- At the time you import data from S3, it may overwrite your items in the DynamoDB table, and exporting data from DynamoDB may overwrite data in the S3 bucket
- Import and export will consume some provisioned throughput capacity
- Be aware of the cost while importing and exporting as it will create an EMR cluster for computation

Now, you are ready to import data from the DynamoDB console. Follow the given procedure:

1. Go to your DynamoDB console and on the **Tables** screen click on your DynamoDB table, and then click on the **Import Table** button.
2. On the **Import Table** screen, read the terms and conditions carefully, and to proceed further, check **I have read the walkthrough** and then select **Build a Pipeline**.

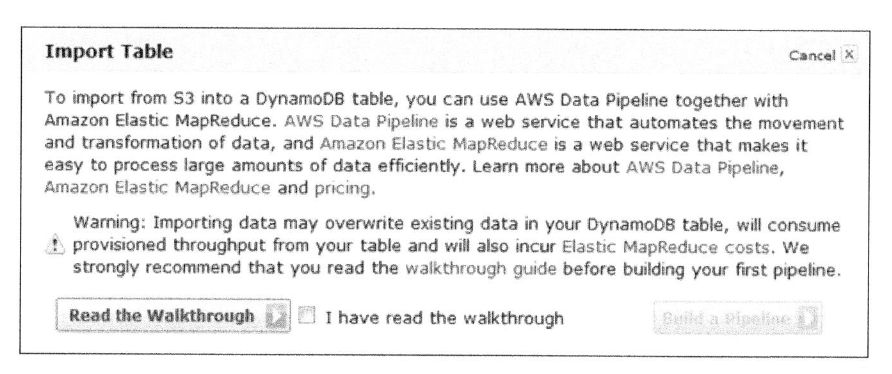

3. It will open the AWS Data Pipeline console as seen previously. So, you can select a template and import your table from DynamoDB.

Creating Data Pipeline

To create a pipeline, you need to consider the following steps:

1. After configuring your pipeline as previously mentioned, you have to choose your template.
2. On the pipeline window, click on **Templates**, and then select **Export S3 to DynamoDB**. Have a look at the following screenshot:

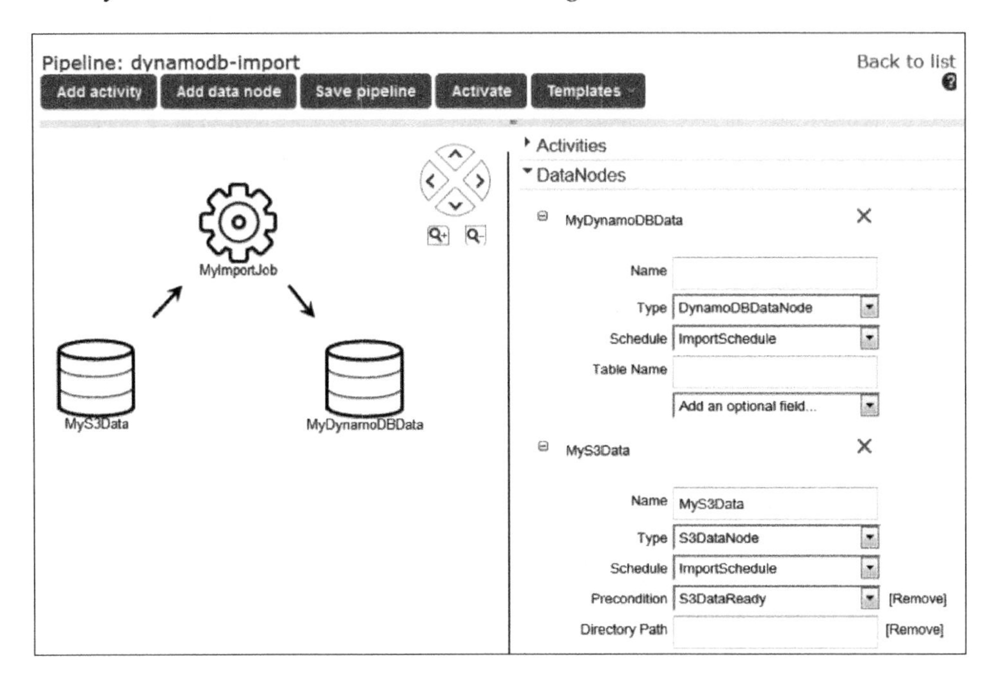

3. You can also enable scheduling for your Data Pipeline, and you can set **ImportSchedule** to 1 hour, for example.
4. Complete the data node objects in your pipeline definition template. For example, in the **DataNodes** pane select the **MyDynamoDB** section; in **Table name**, type your table name where you want to save your output data.
5. To configure your S3 data node, go through the **MyS3Data** section and in **Directory Path**, provide your valid S3 path with the location of your data source.

6. Complete your EMR Cluster, and fill in the EMR **Activities** field. Some fields will be autogenerated by the template, so you need to complete only the remaining ones.
7. Configure the notification action using SNS for AWS Data Pipeline, which must be performed based on the outcome of the activity.

To configure SNS, go through the following steps that will be helpful for your configuration:

1. On the Data Pipeline page, on the right-hand side pane, click on **Others**.
2. On the **Others** pane, go to **LateSnsAlarmsection**, and in **Arn**, enter the ARN of your Amazon SNS topic that you have already created.
3. In the same way, you should create notifications for **FailureSnsAlarm** and **SuccessSnsAlarm**.
4. Validate your configuration and settings, and proceed further by clicking on **Activate**.
5. You will get a confirmation box similar to the following screenshot:

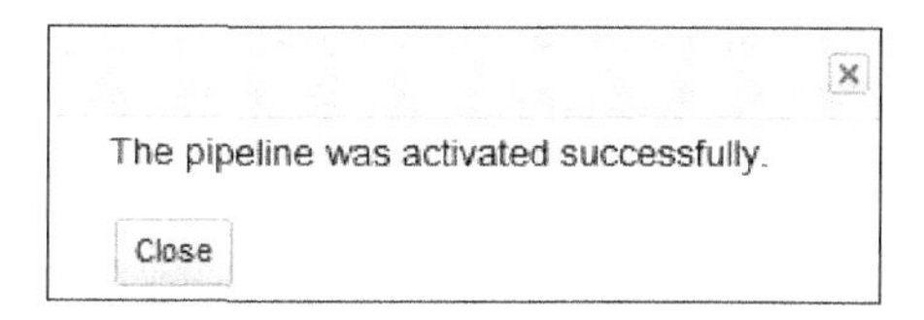

6. Monitor the progress of your pipeline using the console by clicking on **View instance details**.
7. Verify your data import process. For verification, open the DynamoDB console and on the **Tables** screen, click on the DynamoDB table, and then click on the **Explore** button.

   On the **Browse Items** tab, columns that correspond to the data input file should be displayed.

Now you have successfully completed the importing process, and in the same way, you can start exporting the pipeline on your own, because all the steps are very similar to the import process.

Exporting, importing, querying, and joining tables using AWS MapReduce

In this section, you will learn how to use **Amazon Elastic MapReduce** (**Amazon EMR**) with a tailored version of Apache Hive that includes connectivity to DynamoDB to execute operations on data stored in DynamoDB. You can find more information about Apache Hive at `https://hive.apache.org/`. You will perform actions such as the following:

- Loading DynamoDB data tables into the **Hadoop Distributed File System** (**HDFS**)
- Querying live DynamoDB data
- Joining data stored in DynamoDB and exporting or querying it

With Amazon EMR and Hive, you can quickly and efficiently process large amounts of data, such as the data stored in DynamoDB. Apache Hive is a layer that you can use to query a MapReduce cluster using an easy, SQL-like query language called HiveQL. It runs on the Hadoop architecture. To start with the earlier operations, you will have to launch the EMR cluster, specify the location of the DynamoDB tables, and provide the Hive command to manipulate data. There are many ways to start with the EMR cluster. Some of them are:

- Using the management console
- Using CLI
- Using an SDK or API

Hive can be used to test query performance and to tune your application. First you have to set up Hive, and once it's done you can create a Hive script that Amazon EMR can run. There are certain prerequisites that should be fulfilled at the beginning to make Amazon EMR interact with DynamoDB. They are as follows:

- A DynamoDB table
- An adapted version of Hive that includes connectivity to DynamoDB
- Support for DynamoDB connectivity
- Amazon S3 bucket (optional)
- EC2 key pair (optional)

Let's start with them one by one.

Step 1 - Creating a key pair

To interact with EC2 machines launched by Amazon EMR, you will need a key pair.

To generate a key pair, perform the following steps:

1. Click on **Key Pairs** in the navigation pane as shown in the following screenshot:

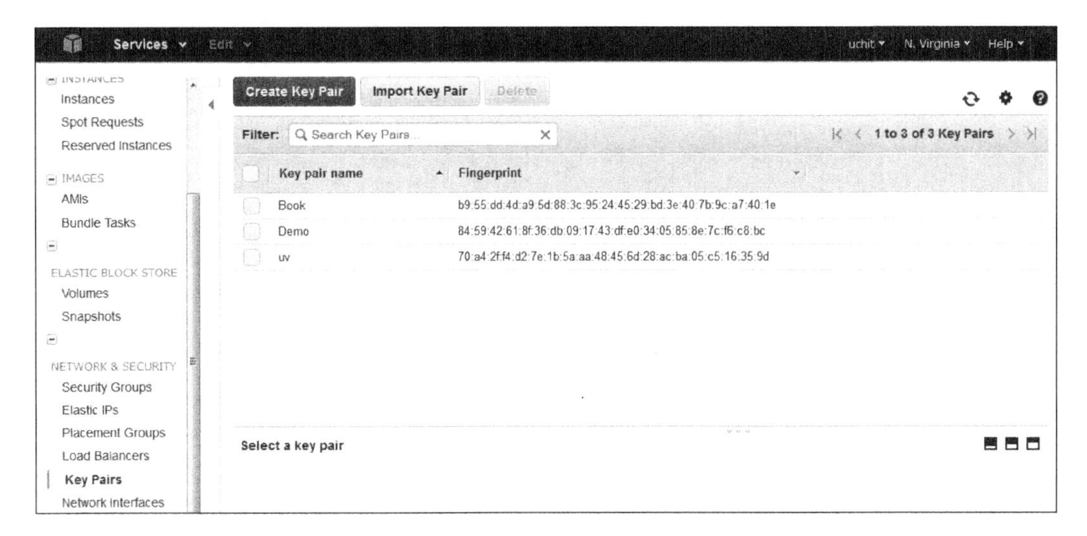

2. You can use your existing key pairs, or you can create a new one from here as described in the screenshot.

[At any point of time, if you lose the key pair, you cannot connect to your Amazon EC2 instances.]

Step 2 - Creating the Amazon EMR cluster

To run Hive on Amazon EMR, you have to create a cluster that has Hive enabled. This configuration needs specific apps and infrastructure to connect with DynamoDB using Hive. The following procedure will explain to you the necessary steps to create and launch an interactive Hive cluster from the AWS management console:

1. Go to Amazon EMR service and click on **Create Cluster**.

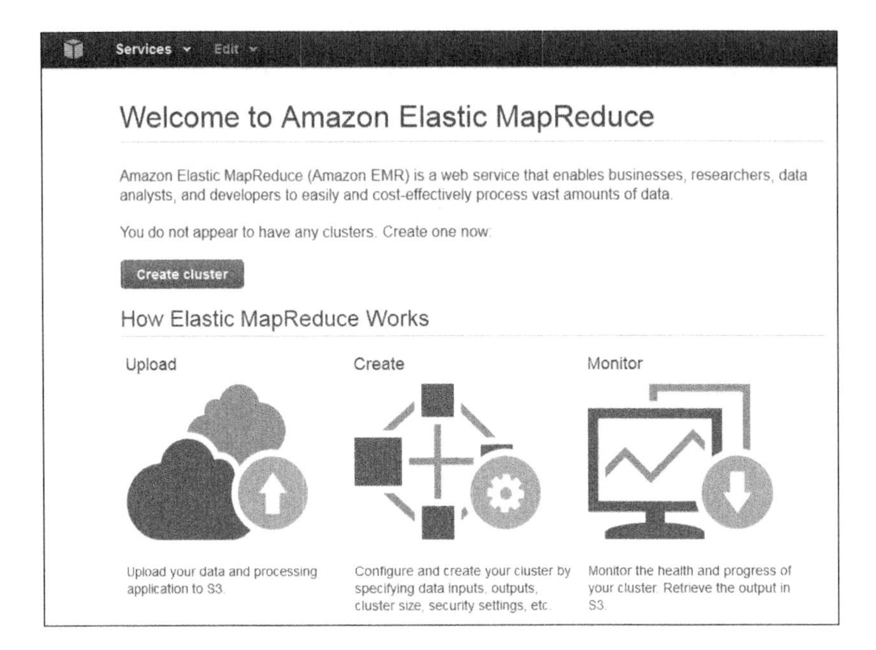

2. On the **Cluster Configuration** page, provide your cluster details, such as **Cluster name**, **Log folder S3 location**, **Debugging**, **Termination protection**, and so on, and click on **Next**. Have a look at the following screenshot:

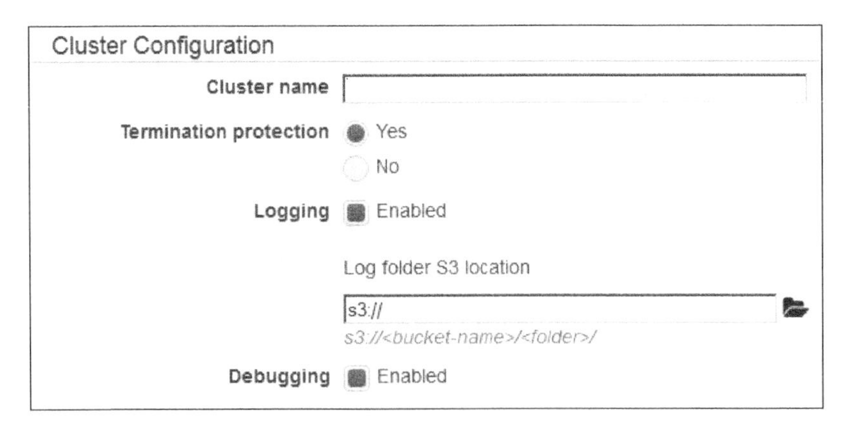

3. On the **Software Configuration** page, verify the fields according to your selection and use case. In the **Applications to be installed** section, if **Hive** and **Pig** are not displayed, select them from the **Additional applications** list. Have a look at the following screenshot:

4. On the **Hardware Configuration** page, verify the details and proceed further. Here the master node assigns Hadoop tasks to core and task nodes and monitors their status within the time interval. Core nodes will be managed by the master node itself, and the core node will be an EC2 instance, which will run the Hadoop map and reduce tasks and store data using the HDFS. Have a look at the following screenshot:

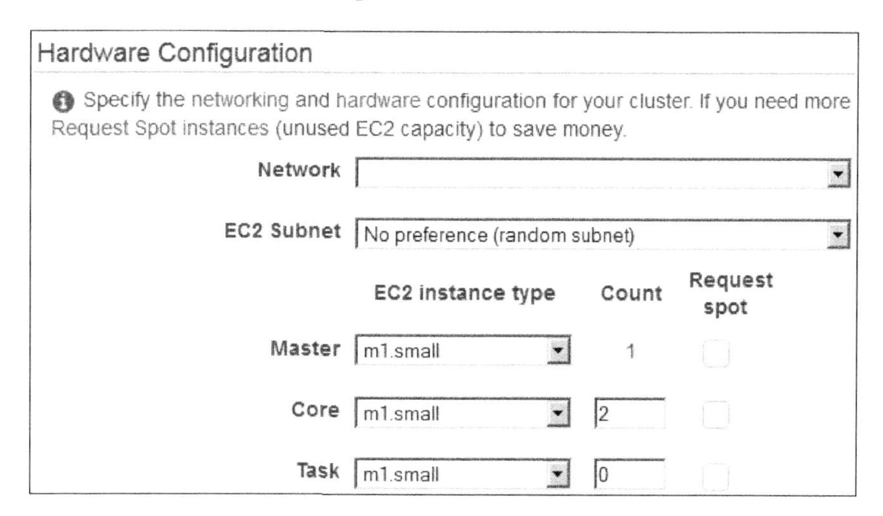

5. On the **Security and Access** page, provide your key pairs and proceed without any roles/IAM user access:

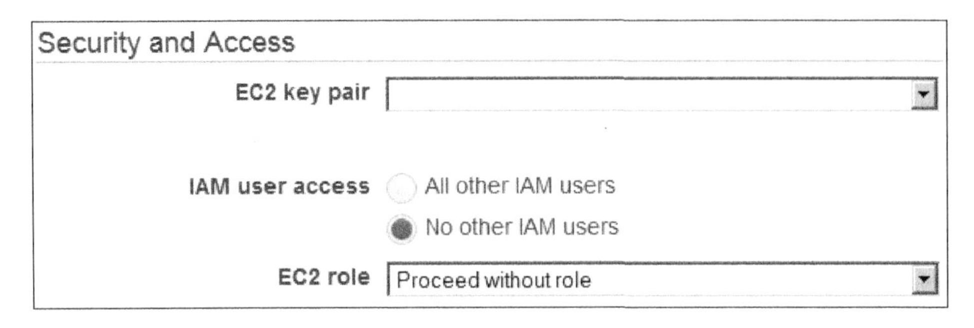

6. Review the configuration, and if it looks okay, simply click on the **Create Cluster** button. It will take some time and will launch the cluster based on your configuration that you can see on the Amazon EMR dashboard.

Step 3 - Connecting the master node via SSH

When the cluster status is **WAITING**, it means the master node is ready for connection. By connecting SSH to the master node, you can perform a CLI operation on the master node.

Step 4 - Setting up the Hive table to run Hive interactive commands

Hive is a data warehousing application, and you can leverage it to use query data in the Amazon EMR clusters using the HiveQL language. To run Hive commands, follow the given steps:

1. On the Hadoop prompt at the master node, type `hive`.
2. You will see a Hive prompt as follows:

```
hive>
```

3. Use the Hive command, which will map a table in the Hive application to the data of DynamoDB. That table will act as a reference entity for the data stored in DynamoDB. The data won't be stored locally on Hive. Check the following command for your reference:

```
CREATE EXTERNAL TABLE hiveuchit (col1 string, col2 bigint,
col3 array<string>)
STORED BY
'org.apache.hadoop.hive.dynamodb.DynamoDBStorageHandler'
TBLPROPERTIES ("dynamodb.table.name" = "dynamodbuchit",
"dynamodb.column.mapping" =
"col1:name,col2:year,col3:holidays");
```

While you are running Hive queries on the DynamoDB table, you have to ensure that you have provided enough read capacity units.

Now you have successfully completed the set up and configuration of EMR with DynamoDB. We will now see some advanced Hive commands to perform operations such as exporting, importing, querying, and joining.

Exporting data from DynamoDB to S3

Using the following command, `s3://bucketname/path/subpath/` is a valid path in your Amazon S3 bucket. Match the columns and data types in the `CREATE` command to go with the values in your DynamoDB tables. Have a look at the following command:

```
CREATE EXTERNAL TABLE yourHiveTableName (col1 string, col2 bigint,
col3 array<string>)
STORED BY 'org.apache.hadoop.hive.dynamodb.DynamoDBStorageHandler'
TBLPROPERTIES ("yourdynamodb.table.name" = "uchit",
"dynamodb.column.mapping" =
"col1:givenname,col2:givenyear,col3:givendays");
```

After that, you can provide the `INSERT OVERWRITE` command to write the data to an external directory/folder.

```
INSERT OVERWRITE DIRECTORY 's3://bucketname/path/' SELECT * FROM
givenHiveTableName;
```

Exporting the DynamoDB table to HDFS

Using the next Hive command, you can perform faster export operations, because Hive 0.7.1.1 will use HDFS as an intermediate step at the time of exporting data to S3. In this example, `hdfs:///directoryName` should be a valid HDFS path, and a table called `givenHiveTableName`, which references DynamoDB, should exist in Hive. Have a look at the following command:

```
CREATE EXTERNAL TABLE givenHiveTableName (col1 string, col2 bigint,
col3 array<string>)
STORED BY 'org.apache.hadoop.hive.dynamodb.DynamoDBStorageHandler'
TBLPROPERTIES ("yourdynamodb.table.name" = "uchit",
"dynamodb.column.mapping" =
"col1:givenname,col2:givenyear,col3:givendays");
INSERT OVERWRITE DIRECTORY 'hdfs:///directoryName' SELECT * FROM
givenHiveTableName;
```

Importing data to DynamoDB

The write capacity should be greater than the number of mappers in the EMR cluster while Hive puts data into DynamoDB. If the capacity is not more than the mappers, it may be that the Hive operation will consume all the write throughput, or try to consume more throughput than is provisioned. Perform the following steps:

1. To import a table from S3 to DynamoDB, you can use the following command:

```
CREATE EXTERNAL TABLE uchit_s3_import(aa_col string, bb_col
bigint, cc_col array<string>)
ROW FORMAT DELIMITED FIELDS TERMINATED BY ','
LOCATION 's3://bucketname/path/subpath/';


CREATE EXTERNAL TABLE givenHiveTableName (col1 string, col2
bigint, col3 array<string>)
STORED BY
'org.apache.hadoop.hive.dynamodb.DynamoDBStorageHandler'
TBLPROPERTIES ("dynamodb.table.name" = "uchit",
"dynamodb.column.mapping" =
"col1:givenname,col2:givenyear,col3:givendays");


INSERT OVERWRITE TABLE 'givenHiveTableName' SELECT * FROM
Uchit_s3_import;
```

2. To import a table from HDFS to DynamoDB, use the following command:

```
CREATE EXTERNAL TABLE Uchit_hdfs_import(aa_col string, bb_col
bigint, cc_col array<string>)
ROW FORMAT DELIMITED FIELDS TERMINATED BY ','
LOCATION 'hdfs:///directoryName';


CREATE EXTERNAL TABLE givenHiveTableName (col1 string, col2
bigint, col3 array<string>)
STORED BY
'org.apache.hadoop.hive.dynamodb.DynamoDBStorageHandler'
TBLPROPERTIES ("dynamodb.table.name" = "uchit",
"dynamodb.column.mapping" =
"col1:givenname,col2:givenyear,col3:givendays");


INSERT OVERWRITE TABLE 'givenhiveTableName' SELECT * FROM
uchit_hdfs_import;
```

Querying data in DynamoDB

There are multiple methods to query your data in DynamoDB. In this section, you will learn the mapping method. The following example will find the largest order placed by a given consumer:

```
CREATE EXTERNAL TABLE my_purchases(consumerId bigint, total_cost
double, items_purchased array<String>)
STORED BY 'org.apache.hadoop.hive.dynamodb.DynamoDBStorageHandler'
TBLPROPERTIES ("dynamodb.table.name" = "Purchases",
"dynamodb.column.mapping" =
"consumerId:ConsumerId,total_cost:Cost,items_purchased:Items");


SELECT max(total_cost) from my_purchases where consumerId = 666;
```

Joining two DynamoDB tables

The following example will map two different Hive tables stored in DynamoDB. It will then call a join within those two tables. The join will be computed on the EMR cluster and will return the computational result based on the join query from the two tables. For real-time scenarios, it may happen that you have to get data from different tables and divide your data into multiple tables. In that case, `JOIN` will be best suited to work with data that resides in multiple tables. So, in this example, you will understand the flow of listing consumers and the purchases of consumers who have placed more than four orders:

```
CREATE EXTERNAL TABLE my_purchases(consumerId bigint, total_cost
double, items_purchased array<String>)
STORED BY 'org.apache.hadoop.hive.dynamodb.DynamoDBStorageHandler'
TBLPROPERTIES ("dynamodb.table.name" = "uchit",
"dynamodb.column.mapping" =
"consumerId:ConsumerId,total_cost:Cost,items_purchased:Items");


CREATE EXTERNAL TABLE givenhive_consumers(consumerId bigint,
consumerName string, consumerResidentialAddress array<String>)
STORED BY 'org.apache.hadoop.hive.dynamodb.DynamoDBStorageHandler'
TBLPROPERTIES ("dynamodb.table.name" = "uchit",
```

```
"dynamodb.column.mapping" =
"consumerId:ConsumerId,consumerName:Name,consumerResidentialAddress:
Address");


Select u.consumerId, u.consumerName, count(*) as count from
givenhive_consumers u
JOIN my_purchases p ON u.consumerId=p.consumerId
GROUP BY u.consumerId, u.consumerName HAVING count > 4;
```

Summary

In this chapter, we have learned about using DynamoDB with other AWS services, such as Amazon EMR, Amazon S3, and Amazon Redshift. We have also discussed how to export, import, query, and join tables using AWS MapReduce with DynamoDB.

In the next chapter, we will learn about advanced DynamoDB with best practices and use cases. We will also learn some basics of uniform workload and time series tables in DynamoDB.

9
DynamoDB – Best Practices

In the previous chapter, we learned about using DynamoDB with other AWS services such as Amazon EMR, Amazon S3, and Amazon Redshift. We also discussed exporting, importing, querying, and joining tables using AWS Elastic MapReduce with DynamoDB.

In this chapter, we will learn the best design use case architectures for DynamoDB. We will also learn real-time problem statements and their best possible solutions. The list of topics that will be covered in the chapter is as follows:

- DynamoDB use cases
- Real-time problem statements and their solutions
- AWS DynamoDB on mobile
- Uniform workload
- Time series tables

As a part of our discussion in this chapter, you will learn about all of these topics. So let's start the journey with the first topic, which will be the DynamoDB use cases.

DynamoDB use cases

There are multiple benefits of using AWS DynamoDB, for example:

- Easy administration
- Schema-less
- Fast and predictable performance
- Scalable
- High availability and durability
- Built-in fault tolerance
- Integrated monitoring

Amazon DynamoDB is a popular product of AWS. The first specific reason might be the price for in-memory technology being cut significantly, both for SSD flash memory and traditional RAM. There are a couple of good use cases in which Amazon DynamoDB has proven to be the best choice and solution. So let's talk about some of the use cases and solutions in particular.

Schema-less-ISH

DynamoDB provides a schema-less service from AWS but the keys have a very big impact on application design, throughput performance, and cost. Let's define what schema-less-ISH is and what kind of work it will do with your DynamoDB tables. So here if you have your hash and range keys, and if you want to use the API, you should query the hash key and range key:

Hash key	8			9			10		
Range key	X	Y	Z	X	Y	Z	X	Y	Z

Table 9.0 – Key table

From the previous table, you can query for all items where `hash == 8`, or all items where `hash == 8` and `range > Y`. However, here you can't perform an API query for all items where `range > Y`; for that, you have to do an expensive table scan.

You can take advantage of the key structure by creating relationships between arbitrary entities on a web application. So, any end user can go on the website and become a "member" or "follower" of the respective article or content. For this kind of scenario we can create the following table for the key schema:

Hash key	**Range key**
content_type.entity_id	FOLLOWER_OF.content_type.entity_id
content_type.entity_id	FOLLOWED_BY.content_type.entity_id

Table 9.1 – Key scheme table

For every relationship you can create two writes; one in each direction of the graph. So using the BOTO library it will look something like the following code:

```
results = table.query(hash_key=user_id,
  range_key=BEGINS_WITH('FOLLOWER_OF.Article.'))
```

Batch applications

For data concentrated applications, for example, applications that are targeted by the Hadoop platform, it is easy to scale the bandwidth and you can simply add more servers to the cluster to scale out the throughput, given that it is reasonable to get an elevated bandwidth both through in-memory technology and through disk-based technology by using horizontal scaling. The very famous project called RAMCloud has made some arguments such as:

- In-memory technology is cheaper in certain use cases
- Hard drive prices also come down year by year

If you wish to admit each data item more commonly, you simply cannot fill up the disk; you will throttle the disk IO interface. You can only utilize a small portion of an HDD if you need high IO throughput, which will definitely take your effective cost per bit up. At various points it will be costlier than an in-memory solution. If you are going to deploy your own infrastructure where you are bearing the entire infrastructure cost, it may make sense to use the in-memory technique for batch applications. However, for hosted cloud environments where you are willing to pay for the actual storage you use, an in-memory technique such as AWS DynamoDB may be the right candidate for your batch applications, but again it's based on your application and cost.

Stating attributes using the :select option

Design your tests table with a compound primary key. The `:hash_value` function will be a UUID of the user and the `:range_value` will be the timestamp, which will be the start time of the test. For such tables in DynamoDB, you can use the query API to query the test items. It will consume some options and the `:hash_value` function will be required. You can either specify different kinds of range values or use the `:limit` option to filter down the tests that you want to retrieve from the table.

In your initial implementation, you can do something similar to what is given in the following code:

```
uchittests = items.query(
  :hash_value => "user UUID",
  :scan_index_forward => false,
  :limit => 10)

uchittests.each do |test|
  render test.attributes.to_h
end
```

The previous code will salvage the last 10 tests run by a user. It will offer the necessary results, but it is unexpectedly slow in my case. The `aws-sdkgems` function will lazy load the attributes for each item by default. So, here you can call `test.attributes.to_h`, which will trigger a new request to DynamoDB to retrieve each attribute. In all it will make `1 + 10 * num_attributes` requests to retrieve your data!

To resolve this you can use the `:select` option to state the attributes you require:

```
uchittests = items.query(
  :hash_value => "user UUID",
  :scan_index_forward => false,
  :limit => 10,
  :select => ['timestamp', 'url', 'response_time'])

uchittests.each do |test|
  render test.attributes['timestamp'],
    test.attributes['url'],
    test.attributes['response_time']
end
```

Now the previous code can retrieve all the attributes within a single request. With this change, you can test that the total load time will be reduced from as much as 9 seconds to a few hundred milliseconds.

Synchronization

With Amazon DynamoDB, you can design solutions for a web session data store. It can be used for highly scalable web applications that require thousands of concurrent requests/sec with persistent session data and specific cache data necessities. Because the web session data is usually within the range of only some bytes to some KBs, it can be easily handled in DynamoDB. It is recommended to use *strong consistent reads* while transacting with session data in DynamoDB. The following is the reference diagram for data synchronization:

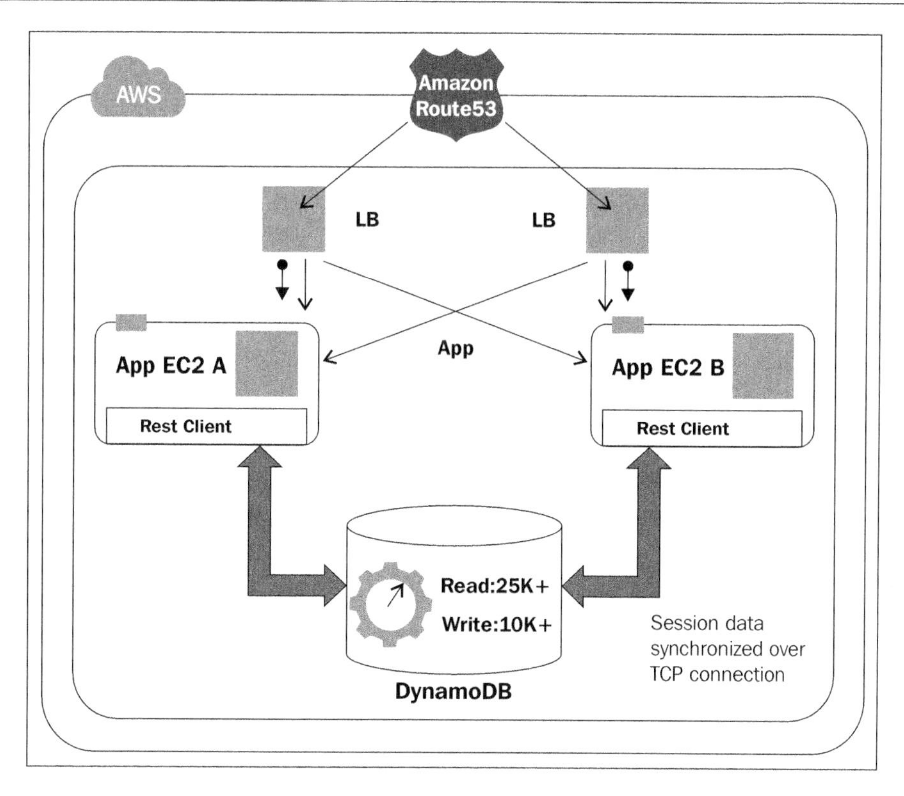

Real-time problem statements and their solutions

DynamoDB was designed to serve each and every need of Amazon.com. DynamoDB can handle extreme fluctuations in volume as those can occur during peak hours or the holiday season with single-bit latency for reads and writes.

Problem statement – 1

Let's first take an example of one of the start-up companies providing video monitoring hardware and software to their customers. Initially the company has developed its own storage solution, which proved to be time consuming, and they had to spend time architecting their storage solution, which also made it difficult to scale. Their customers can view high-definition video which can be viewed from iOS and Android devices or the Internet. Consumers and small businesses can use the company's video platform to monitor homes, offices, or pets. The company offers a free trial, real-time streaming service as well as **Cloud Video Recording** (**CVR**), a subscription service that gives their users the ability to review stored footage over a 7 or 30-day period and make clips. Their major problem was to maintain provisioned throughput and streaming.

Solution

As a solution the company has considered other cloud providers. The company chose AWS because of cost effectiveness and the maturity of AWS solutions. The company runs their video streaming services and storage servers on Amazon-managed EC2 and Amazon S3, and uses Amazon DynamoDB to scale and maintain throughput for customers, as they were suffering because of their provisioned throughput and managing the large data sets of their customers. Now the company's developers don't have to work hard writing code and database queries such as write queries, and they report consistent low latency with DynamoDB.

Problem statement – 2

Somebody was developing a freelancer platform for certain professionals. That developer was thinking of utilizing AWS DynamoDB for logging user activity (such as posting a job, hiring professionals, and so on). So he has done some work and selected some fields like the ones in the following code:

```
user_id
ip_address
timestamp
data
```

After selecting these fields, he will be querying DynamoDB for the following information:

- Log of activity by selected users
- Log of all the user activity performed at a certain hour or on a certain day

The information will have to be saved and accessible for a long time. Now the question is: how good will DynamoDB be for this kind of scenario?

Solution

DynamoDB is very famous for its high-performance retrieval. Basically, it uses **solid-state drive (SSD)**, so storage prices may be a little bit expensive if you are going to store that data forever on it when talking about high volumes. Hence, Amazon DynamoDB can be the perfect solution for you and the preferred solution for schema can be as follows:

```
hash_key = <user_id>:YYYY-MM-DD
range_key = full_ISO_8601_timestamp
ip_address
data
```

Here, `ISO_8601` is all the time a superior initiative if you need to sort the dates.

The developer can even append the date to the `user_id` function to make queries easier and to keep things logically grouped, but it will be complex for more advanced queries. So, as a solution you can avoid that complexity by using the `BETWEEN` filter of `Query`.

Let's take another example of a company that offers a full suite of data protection and management solutions for enterprise laptops, PCs, smartphones, and tablets.

Problem statement – 3

To expand their business and to meet the demands of their customers who want a cloud-based solution, the company decided to offer a cloud version of their application platform. They had linear scalability with no resort to designing and building systems themselves to get the desired throughput for their platform.

Solution

AWS offered different services and Amazon DynamoDB allowed the company to decrease Amazon EC2 instances by 75 percent and reduce costs by 30 percent.

The following is the reference architectural diagram for the problem statement. Managing the database and their tables for data was a headache for the company. So it has moved away from the Cassandra database that it was using and expanded its cloud stack to include Amazon DynamoDB.

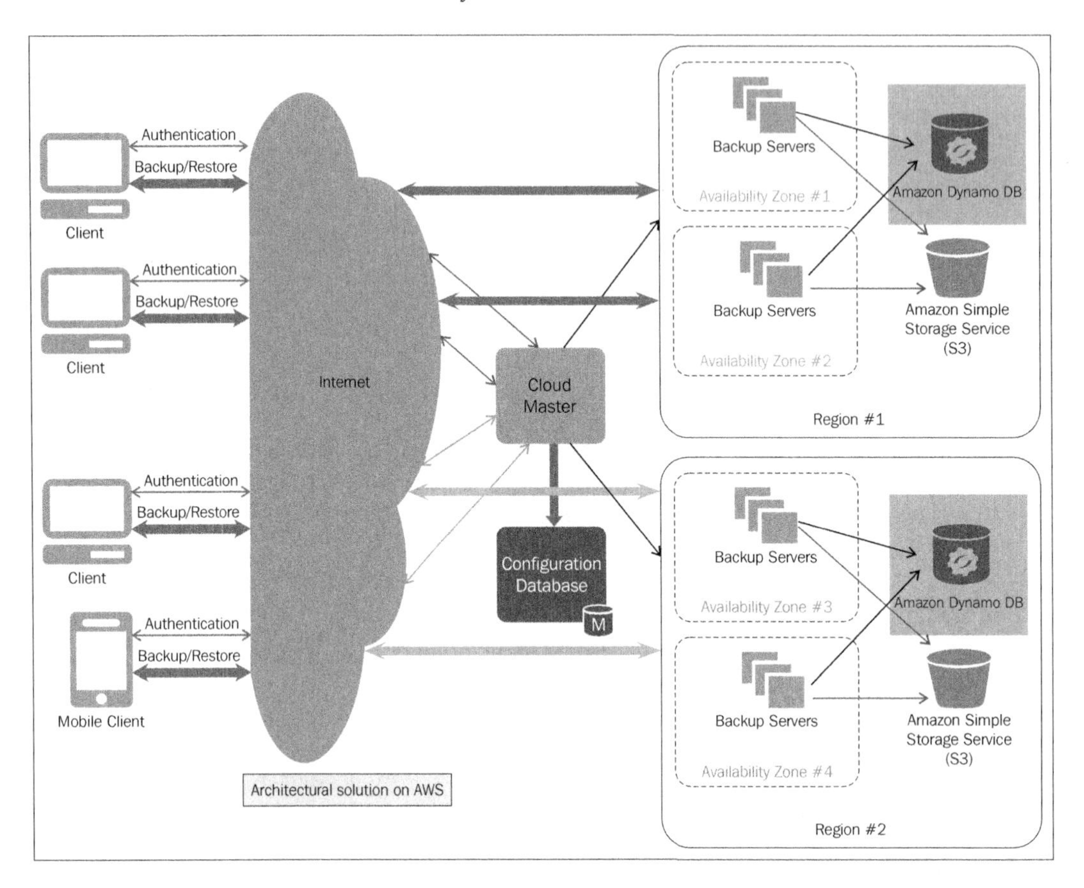

Let's discuss another case study in which the company provides cross-platform reach across large display inventory sources and tools that personalize advertisement campaigns based on a visitor's browsing behavior.

Problem Statement – 4

Since the company X was developing real-time bidding infrastructure, it needed to sync the data of each user across multiple regions, with hundreds of millions of users and tens of thousands of writes per second. The company's bidding system has a hard cap of 100 milliseconds for every bid request, so the company needs strong assurances on the read performance.

Solution

After evaluating multiple substitutes, the company decided on DynamoDB for its low latency, guaranteed throughput, and ability to scale quickly across multiple regions. So their database tables were designed to use the cookie as the hash key and profile ID as the range key with timestamp as the attribute, as given in the following table:

Hash key	Range key	Attribute
User ID	User profile	Timestamp
"4321"	"part1"	"09979894867"
"4321"	"part2"	"09979894872"

Table 9.2 - Unique table

Right now, the company has created the DynamoDB client and they are just writing to it, measuring the write throughput and read throughput and getting the benefits without having to dive into the details. By using Amazon DynamoDB in conjunction with Apache Storm, the company is replicating their important data set across the globe within 50 milliseconds for high availability, providing speedy response times for both bidding and serving up ads to customers—while keeping costs low, with low latency and higher throughput.

Let's discuss another case study in which the company has created a mobile communications application that brings a walkie-talkie functionality to iOS and Android devices. With that application customers can make real-time, push-to-talk calls with one person or a group of people at the same time, regardless of the distance.

Problem statement – 5

The application was a great success and reached 1 million users within the first two and a half months, so the company had to scramble to meet the demand. In the beginning, the company experienced scaling issues because of the way they designed the application. However, AWS gives us the right building blocks. It was confusing for the company to design correctly and build the system in a correct way. They struggled with a lot of manual work to optimize the relational database service to serve their users on a massive scale.

Solution

When Amazon DynamoDB became available on the market, the company's technical team built new storage-dependent infrastructure components on DynamoDB for their application to take advantage of the highly scalable database service. The given architecture diagram was the proposed success solution:

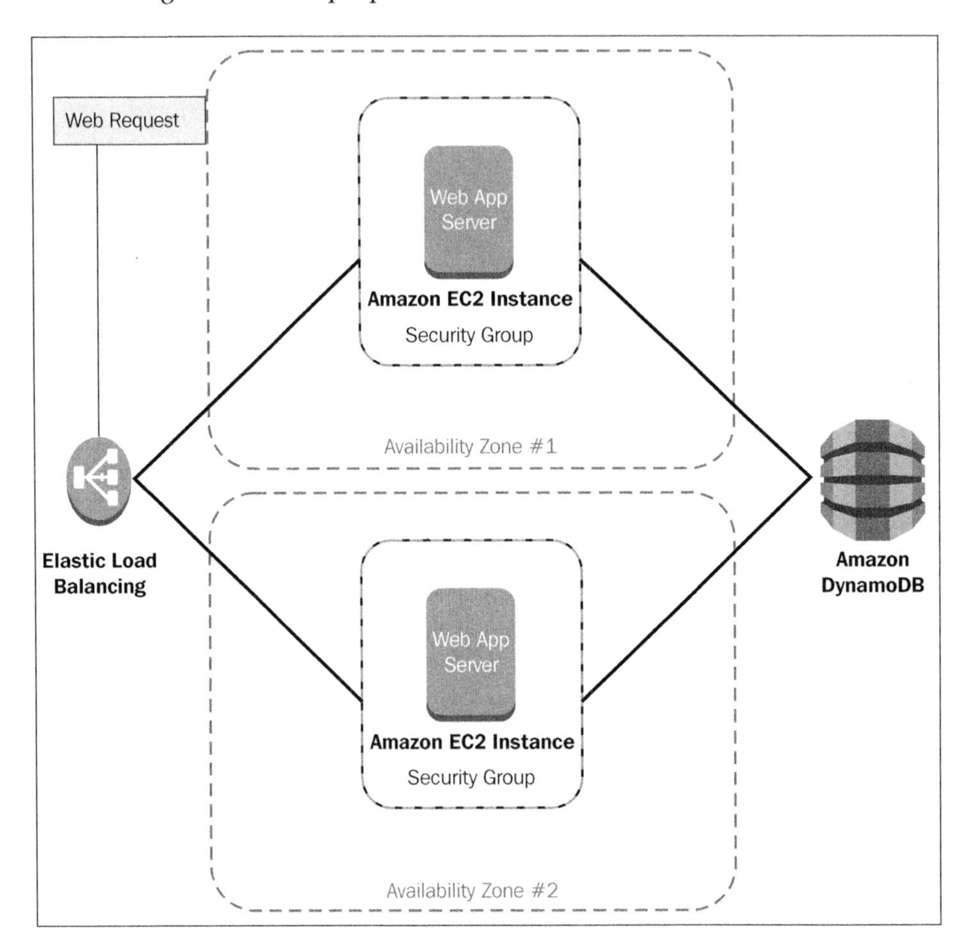

AWS DynamoDB on mobile

Amazon DynamoDB, as we have seen, is a rapidly-growing service from the AWS services stack. It is a fully-managed database service for the NoSQL database category. All the data items are stored in SSDs and will automatically be replicated with different **Availability Zones** (**AZs**) for **High Availability** (**HA**) and durability of data. Using Amazon DynamoDB, you can create and manage mobile applications along with the help of AWS Mobile SDKs.

AWS Mobile SDK will give you full freedom to access DynamoDB for your queries, to create tables and more, over all basics of the **CRUD (Create, Read, Update, Delete)** operations within table. So in this example, you will learn the coding mechanism for both Android as well as iOS mobile platforms.

Storing data in the table

Let's take a look at a table where you want to store some data about the user, such as a first name, his/her location, and his/her highest exam score. You can create the table in many ways, but here you will go through the following way which is much easier in DynamoDB. Try to remember the first four chapters in which you learned about hash keys and range keys. You are going to use those fundamentals here frequently. So assume that your first look of the table will be like this:

BookID	**RecordID**	**Data**
4321	bookname	DynamoDB
4321	location	Gujarat, India
4321	copies	2000
9876	bookname	EC2
9876	location	Seattle, WA
9876	copies	3400

Table 9.3 – Book data table

Here, your `BookId` function will be your hash key to recognize the book uniquely, which will be stored as a numeric value. The `RecordId` function will work as your range key to recognize the record corresponding with the book and will be stored as a string. The `Data` field will work as the actual record for the books. In this example, you will learn for both platforms: iOS and Android.

To load specific data, follow the given code for iOS and Android.

Android

The following code is used to load specific data for Android:

```
Map<String, AttributeValue> key = new HashMap<String,
AttributeValue>();
key.put("BookId", 4321);
key.put("RecordId", "bookname");

GetItemRequest getItemRequest = new
  GetItemRequest("BookTableExample",key);
```

```
GetItemResult getItemResult = ddbClient.getItem(getItemRequest);

Log.i(LOG_TAG, "value1 = '"+
  getItemResult.getItem().get("bookname").getS() + "'");
```

iOS

The following code is used to load specific data for iOS:

```
DynamoDBGetItemRequest *getItemRequest =
  [DynamoDBGetItemRequest new];
getItemRequest.tableName = @"BookTableExample";

DynamoDBAttributeValue *bookId = [[DynamoDBAttributeValuealloc]
  initWithN:@"4321"];
DynamoDBAttributeValue *recordId = [[DynamoDBAttributeValuealloc]
  initWithS:@"bookname"];
getItemRequest.key =
  [NSMutableDictionarydictionaryWithObjectsAndKeys:userId,
  @"bookId", recordId, @"RecordId", nil];

DynamoDBGetItemResponse *getItemResponse =
  [self.ddbgetItem:getItemRequest];

DynamoDBAttributeValue *name =
  [getItemResponse.itemvalueForKey:@"Data"];
NSLog(@"book name = '%@'", bookname.s);
```

So if you know the record to load, you can use the `GetItem` API to fetch the record by its associated primary key and pull your data from the results.

Updating a record

In the same way, if you want to update a record in table you can try the `PutItem` API action. You can use any value type; so choose an attribute in the item. However, by mixing and matching attribute types, you will be able to select the required one.

Android

The following code is used to update a record for Android:

```
Map<String,AttributeValue> item = new HashMap
  <String, AttributeValue>();
item.put("BookId",
  new AttributeValue().withN("4321"));
```

```
item.put("RecordId",
  new AttributeValue().withS("FavoriteBooks"));

item.put("Data",
  new AttributeValue().withSS("Computer", "Science", "Physics"));


PutItemRequest putItemRequest = new
  PutItemRequest("BookTableExample", item);

// process the request
PutItemResult putItemResult = ddbClient.putItem(putItemRequest);
```

iOS

The following code is used to update a record for iOS:

```
DynamoDBPutItemRequest *putItemRequest =
  [DynamoDBPutItemRequest new];
request.tableName = @"BookTableExample";

DynamoDBAttributeValue *value = [[DynamoDBAttributeValuealloc]
  initWithN:@"4321"];
[request.itemsetValue:valueforKey:@"BookId"];

value = [[DynamoDBAttributeValuealloc]
  initWithS:@"FavoriteBooks"];
[request.itemsetValue:valueforKey:@"RecordId"];

value = [DynamoDBAttributeValue new];
[valueaddSS:@"Computer"];
[valueaddSS:@"Science"];
[valueaddSS:@"Physics"];
[request.itemsetValue:valueforKey:@"Data"];

// process the request
DynamoDBPutItemResponse *response = [self.ddbputItem:request];
```

Deleting a record

To delete a record from the table, you can use the `DeleteItem` API action, which will only require you to pass the key of the item you want to delete.

Android

The following code is used to delete a record for Android:

```
Map<String,AttributeValue> key = new
  HashMap<String,AttributeValue>();
key.put("BookId", new AttributeValue().withN("4321"));
key.put("RecordId", new AttributeValue().withS("FavoriteBooks"));
DeleteItemRequest deleteItemRequest = new DeleteItemRequest("BookTable
Example", key);

// process our request
DeleteItemResult deleteItemResponse =
  ddbClient.deleteItem(deleteItemRequest);
```

iOS

The following code is used to delete a record for iOS:

```
DynamoDBDeleteItemRequest *deleteItemRequest =
  [DynamoDBDeleteItemRequest new];
request.tableName = @"BookTableExample";

DynamoDBAttributeValue *value = [[DynamoDBAttributeValuealloc]
  initWithN:@"4321"];
[deleteItemRequest.keysetValue:valueforKey:@"BookId"];
value = [[DynamoDBAttributeValuealloc]
  initWithS:@"FavoriteColors"];
[deleteItemRequest.keysetValue:valueforKey:@"RecordId"];

DynamoDBDeleteItemResponse *deleteItemResponse =
  [self.ddbdeleteItem:deleteItemRequest];
```

The previous examples show the basics of writing and modifying data to Amazon DynamoDB with the AWS Mobile SDKs.

Uniform workload

For uniform data access within items in your tables, you have to identify the workload patterns on items/tables. Your provisioned throughput is dependent on the primary key plus pattern of workload on items. At the time of storing data, DynamoDB will divide your items into more than one partition and will distribute your data based on the hash key element. So your throughput will be associated with a table which is also divided among partitions. This throughput will be based on no sharing among all partitions.

To get the quantity of requested throughput, you have to keep your workload spread out evenly among the hash key values. By distributing the hash key values, you can distribute the requests across multiple partitions.

Let's take an example. If your table has a single hash key element for your content, and supposing your hash key element is heavily accessed, the traffic will be concentrated in a small number of partitions. Here you have only one for example. So from the example, you can say that your workload will be heavily unbalanced as it is focused on one partition only, so the operations won't achieve the desired throughput level. To get the desired output as provisioned throughput, you have to build tables in such a way that the hash key element has a huge number of distinct values and it should be fairly random, but with some meaning.

This does not mean that you have to access all the hash keys, but when your workload is accessing more distinctive hash keys be careful that operations will spread across the partitioned space in such a way that it can better utilize your given throughput level. So, there is a simple phenomenon that utilizes the throughput more accurately as the combined ratio of hash keys accessed to total hash keys in a table grows. Now the question is: how to decide on hash keys for the provisioned throughput efficiency? The user ID can be a good example of having good efficiency because any application will have lots of users. On the other hand, for status code, only a few status codes will be available. So based on status code as the hash key value efficiency may be poor. You have to consider your write operations among more different hash values when the number of hash key values are very few in a single table.

For example, let's consider a combined primary hash and range key where the hash key represents a book ID, in which the book ID `U66` is often heavily exhausted with requests. To increase write and read performance for throughput for a particular *hot* hash key, choose a random number from a fixed set (let's say 1 to 400) of `U66.1`, `U66.2` through `U66.300`. Because of this randomness, writes for the book ID `U66` are spread across multiple hash key values for better throughput and parallelism.

This approach seriously fine grains the write throughput, but reads for a specific item become harder because you are not aware of which of the 400 keys contains the particular item. Here, instead of selecting a completely random number, select a number that you will be able to calculate from a bit inherent to the item. Here for example, if the item shows a customer that has the book, calculate the hash key suffix from his/her name or book ID. This calculation should compute a number between 1 and 400 that is reasonably distributed given any set of names (or book IDs.) Now the writes are extending across the hash keys. You can easily perform a `get` operation because you can conclude the related hash key when you want to regain a specific *book consumer* value. Query operations require a tranquil environment to run beside all *U66.x* keys and your app requires specific logic to merge all of the query results for each hash key value. But here, the schema will avoid *hot* hash keys taking all of the workload.

Time series tables

With DynamoDB, when you are creating a table you are going to specify the throughput. So from that DynamoDB will allocate resources to serve your requirements with low latency as best as it can. The core concept is that you should identify the core pattern of your tables that will be accessed via an application and based on that analysis you can restructure your application and tables.

Let's say, for example, you are designing a table to map the customers' search patterns on your application on the Web. So you can design your DynamoDB table with hash and range type primary keys with consumer ID as the hash attribute and date/time as the range attribute. So within this application your customer data will grow indefinitely with time; however, your application will show the uneven access pattern across items given in the table. In this pattern, it is possible that the latest item will be more frequently accessed and eventually the older items will be rarely accessed. So if you get this kind of known pattern and table behavior from the application, you can justify this at the time of designing your schema. Instead of storing each and every item on the same table, you can divide it into multiple tables based on access behavior. You can create tables to store daily or weekly data. On whatever table the data access rate is high, you can request higher throughput on it and for tables that have unaccessed or older data, you can cut down some throughput and save on resources.

So, storing frequently-accessed items called *hot* content with great throughput in one table and rarely accessed items called *cold* items with reduced throughput in another table can help you to save resources. You can even refuse old data items by simply deleting their respective tables, or you can switch that content to another storage service such as S3 for future reference. To delete the whole table will be more efficient than a one-by-one process as it will double the write throughput as you will perform many put operations.

When to use and when not to use DynamoDB

You are almost done with DynamoDB now and this will be the last topic of the book, so here as a best use case I am providing you with a recap of the basics for DynamoDB.

When to use DynamoDB:

- When key-value or simple queries are present
- When a very high read/write rate is needed
- When auto-sharding is required
- When auto-scaling is required
- When low latency is required
- When there is no size or throughput limit
- When there is no tuning
- When high durability is required

When *not* to use DynamoDB:

- When multi-item or cross table transactions are required
- When complex queries and joins are required
- When real-time analytics on historic data is required

Summary

In this chapter, we learned the best design use case architectures for DynamoDB. We also discussed real-time problem statements and their best possible solutions. In this chapter we learned about uniform workload and time series tables.

I hope you enjoyed the DynamoDB journey. A lot more is still pending. You will find more interesting comparisons of DynamoDB with other NoSQL databases in *Appendix, Comparing DynamoDB*.

Comparing DynamoDB

A web-based applications era is in progress everywhere, and through web-based applications, a massive amount of data is getting generated. By leveraging the Amazon DynamoDB platform, you can simply dial up your requirement based on the request capacity of a table, without incurring downtime. Amazon DynamoDB will take care of your entire administrative and management burden, and you can concentrate on your business logic.

With reference to other relational databases' robust characteristics and functionality, it is a very complex and time-consuming process. If your requirements are dynamic and the changes are based on traffic and usage scenarios, plus if you need the desired throughput while accessing data from the database, Amazon DynamoDB will work best for you. So let's make some comparisons with other data storage services that can come under the NoSQL category.

DynamoDB versus MongoDB

Both DynamoDB and MongoDB are NoSQL databases used to build for high scalability, high performance, and high availability. The main difference between the two is that DynamoDB is a service provided by Amazon AWS, so it can only run in AWS. MongoDB is a software application provided by the database company MongoDB Inc (formerly known as 10gen Inc), which can be installed and run anywhere. From the data model point of view, DynamoDB is a key-value database, which means that it's a columnar database, whereas MongoDB is a document-oriented Database. DynamoDB abstracts all the operations details of replication and sharding of the database from the end user, but in MongoDB we have full access to the source code and can dig into the file formats. This might be an advantage or a disadvantage. MongoDB uses internal memory to store the (windowed) working set, enabling faster access to data. So if our datasets are much larger than the accessible memory, then DynamoDB scales to much larger datasets.

DynamoDB is suitable for use cases where data access is by one or two dimensions of data, but if your data access patterns state more than two dimensions of data, then MongoDB is a better option, because it supports any number of indexes. MongoDB has major limitations when running MapReduce jobs, but DynamoDB integrates with **Elastic MapReduce** (**EMR**) and reduces the complexity of analyzing unstructured data.

If you have an AWS account, then DynamoDB is very simple to use, which means that we have to work only on applications, whereas other management of the database server would be handled by AWS. This means that if you have less manpower, then it's good to use DynamoDB. If we use DynamoDB, then other Amazon services, such as CloudSearch, Elastic MapReduce, and other services for database backup and restore can be easily integrated with it so that it can speed up development and reduce the cost of server management. In MongoDB, we must have the right servers, installation, and configurations. AWS provides excellent performance with DynamoDB by giving single-digit latency on very heavy data traffic. All data is replicated synchronously across all availability zones without any downtime, even while there are frequent throughput updates. The Amazon DynamoDB pricing policy is *pay only for what you use*, which means you can buy on operations-per-second capability instead of CPU hours or storage space. You have to specify the request throughput of your table you want to achieve (the capacity you request to reserve for reads and writes). The official AWS SDK supports Java, JavaScript, Ruby, PHP, Python, and .NET, while MongoDB mostly supports the likes of C, C++, Perl, Erlang, PowerShell, ProLog, MATLAB, and so on.

Let's look more closely into the comparison of DynamoDB and MongoDB:

Specification	**DynamoDB**	**MongoDB**
Data model	Key value	Document store
Operating system	Cross platform (hosted)	Linux Windows Solaris OS X
License	Commercial	Open source
Data storage	Solid-state drive (SSD)	Any
Secondary indexes	Yes	Yes
Accessing method	REST API	JSON
Server-side script	No	JavaScript
Triggers	No	No
Partitioning	Sharding	Sharding

Specification	DynamoDB	MongoDB
Integrity model supports	• BASE • MVCC • ACID • Eventual consistency • Log replication • Read committed	BASE
Atomicity	Yes	Conditional
Transaction	No	Yes
Full text search	No	Yes
Geospatial indexes	No	Yes
Horizontal scalability	Yes	Yes
Replication method	Master-slave replica	Master-slave replica
Max. size value	64 KB	16 MB
Object-relational mapping	No	Yes
Function-based index	Yes	No
Log Support	No	Yes
Operation performed per second	1,000	10,000
User concepts	Access rights for users and roles can be defined via the **AWS Identity and Access Management (IAM)**	Users can be defined with full access or read-only access

In the previous table, the Integrity model supports row mentions a few values. They are as follows:

- **BASE**: It stands for Basically Available, Soft state, Eventual consistency
- **MVCC**: It stands for Multiversion Concurrency Control
- **ACID**: It stands for Atomicity, Consistency, Isolation, Durability

DynamoDB versus Cassandra

Let's start with a data model such as DynamoDB's storage model, which is very similar to Cassandra's model, in which data is hashed on the row key, and the data inside the key is ordered by a specific column of the insert. In DynamoDB, a column can be single valued or scalar, which means that attributes can be multivalued. Cassandra has various attribute types, such as `Integer`, `BigInteger`, `ASCII`, `UTF8`, and `Double`, and it also offers composite and dynamic composite columns. It provide the full range of data formats, which include structured, semi-structured and unstructured data that can be run on recent applications, whereas DynamoDB has only two attribute types, namely `String` and `Number`.

Multi-datacenter across all regions is supported by Cassandra, whereas DynamoDB replicates data across multiple availability zones in the same region, but cross-region is not supported. So if we want to provide local data latencies in any regions across the world, then Cassandra provides full control over data consistency.

Let's take a scenario in which we require a large number of increments with a few counters, with the ability to read the current counter. Scaling the throughput on an individual counter is quite difficult, because there is a direct read/write operation performed. So if we need more than one node to handle one count, then the read operation becomes slow, and it involves all the nodes. In this case, we retry this operation in the event, because we don't know whether our previous request succeeded. We are performing the same update twice so that it frequently causes a long latency or load spikes across the cluster. In DynamoDB, there is an atomic counter that is more reliable with low latency, and it supports as many increments as the operations we have performed.

In DynamoDB the overload is effectively handled. If we exceed the predicted/mentioned throughput, we rapidly get the `ThroughputExceeded` error; meanwhile, no other requests are affected. This is very useful for a heavily-loaded site where thousands of requests come at a time, and, because of the latency spikes, queues will be generated with great thrust.

In Cassandra, the virtual node scale-up is pretty easy, but the scale-down operation remains slow, manual, and error prone. In data streaming, the transmitting nodes are joining or leaving the rings. This causes a group failure of nodes, so it requires repairing. Also, data lost during the decommissioning operation requires data restore through a backup. In DynamoDB, scale-up becomes effortless with a single-line command that waits for a while to be scaled, while in Cassandra Cluster, it's a multistep as well as multihour process. In Dynamo DB, scale-down is also better and much less time consuming, with low latency.

DynamoDB has the capability to insert or delete an item from a set without using complex code. Its operational cost will be zero as, once we set up backup jobs at specific time intervals, there is no need to manage the database, no disk space monitoring, no need to check memory usage, and no need to replace or repair the failed node. DynamoDB saves costs too. Cassandra basically supports a logically unlimited amount of data at a time with a specific key. This means that this limit is up to the disk space on a particular node, but DynamoDB's limit is up to 64 KB, so it might be tricky to handle overflow. Cassandra supports transactions very well by delivering ACID compliance using a commit log to capture all read and write operations, with built-in redundancy that ensures data durability if the hardware fails.

Now take a look at the tabular comparison between these two databases:

Specification	DynamoDB	Cassandra
Data model	Key-value store	Key-value with wide column store
Operating system	Cross platform (hosted)	BSD Linux OS X Windows
License	Commercial (Amazon)	Commercial(Apache)
Data storage	Solid-state drive (SSD)	Filesystem
Secondary indexes	Yes	No
Accessing method	API call	API call **CQL** (short for **Cassandra Query Language**) Apache Thrift
Server-side script	No	No
Triggers	No	Yes
Partitioning	Sharding	Sharding
MapReduce	No (can be done with other services of AWS)	Yes
Integrity model supports	• BASE • MVCC • ACID • Eventual consistency • Log replication • Read committed	BASE

Specification	DynamoDB	Cassandra
Composite key support	Yes	Yes
Data consistency	Yes	Most operations
Distributed counters	Yes	Yes
Idempotent write batches	No	Yes
Time to live support	No	Yes
Conditional updates	Yes	No
Indexes on column value	No	Yes
Hadoop integration	M/R, Hive	M/R, Hive, Pig
Monitorable	Yes	Yes
Backups	Low impact snapshot with incremental	incremental
Deployment policy	Only with AWS	Anywhere
Transaction	No	Yes
Full text search	No	No
Geospatial indexes	No	No
Horizontal scalability	Yes	Yes
Replication method	Master-slave replica	Master-slave replica
Largest value supported	64 KB	2 GB
Object-relational mapping	No	Yes
Log support	No	Yes
User concepts	Access rights for users and roles can be defined via **AWS Identity and Access Management (IAM)**	Users can be defined per object

DynamoDB versus S3

DynamoDB and **S3** (short for **Simple Storage Service**) are both storage/database services provided by Amazon to be exposed to the NoSQL database. S3 is used for wide data storage as it has capacity to store data up to a 5 TB maximum item size, where as DynamoDB has capacity to store data up to 64 KB, but both have no limit on attributes for a particular item. S3 creates a bucket that stores data. Buckets are the essential containers in Amazon S3 for data storage. S3 is for large data storage, which we are rarely going to use. For example, data stored for analysis purposes or data stored for the backup and restore procedure. It has a slower response time. DynamoDB is used for high performance. In DynamoDB, we need a key-value data store that can handle thousands of read/write operations per second.

DynamoDB is a flexible NoSQL database that we use to store small features, metadata, and index information—in short, data that is more dynamic. In DynamoDB, data retrieval is very fast because the data is stored on SSDs, and the data is replicated across many servers that are located in availability zones.

While using S3, we don't need to configure anything to get started. We need a key, and we can upload the data; it's the way to store data in S3. Now you only need to keep track of the key we used for a particular application. In DynamoDB, we need to configure a few things, such as when creating tables, we need to specify the primary key as well as make provision for the read/write throughput value. S3 doesn't support object locking, but if we need it, then we have to build it manually, whereas DynamoDB supports optimistic object locking. Optimistic locking is an approach to ensure that the client-side item that we are updating is the same as the item in DynamoDB. If we use this approach, then our database writes are protected from being overwritten by other writes.

One of the good features of S3 is that every S3 object or document that is stored in it has a web address. By using this web address, a document can be accessed without any impact on the web server or the database.

S3 uses the eventual consistency model in which, if no new updates are made on a given data item, all accesses to that item will return the last updated value. DynamoDB follows eventual consistency and strong consistency, in which all accesses are seen by all parallel processes, by all parallel nodes, and by all processors in sequential order. DynamoDB doesn't support spatial data. It can store points and extend it to build a Geohash-based index that also indexes lines (for example, roads) and areas (for example, boundaries) that represent arbitrary area features, which means each Geohash-index record stored in DynamoDB. But we can store this information if it's a small geographical area, otherwise the spatial feature is stored as an object in S3, with a pointer to the S3 location that is stored in DynamoDB.

DynamoDB is presently provisioned completely on SSD devices. SSD devices can read requests in a small fraction of time as compared to a magnetic disk (about 100 times faster) by servicing individual data, though the cost per GB of storage is much higher (approximately 10 times) than that of a magnetic disk. Hence DynamoDB can provide very low latency and high throughput compared to S3 but at a higher cost per unit of storage. Let's take a scenario in which 1 GB of DynamoDB storage costs $1 per month, while S3 storage costs between 4 cents and 12 cents per GB per month. This means it is eight times cheaper than DynamoDB. DynamoDB also provides a flexible fee structure based on the IO capacity. In this, 1,000 read operation per second will cost around 20 cents per hour, and the write operation is about 5 times more expensive, because SSDs can perform a read operation much faster than a write operation.

Now take a look at the tabular comparison between DynamoDB and S3:

Specification	DynamoDB	S3
Data model	Key-value store	Store object/data in bucket
Operating system	Cross platform (hosted)	Cross platform (hosted)
License	Commercial (Amazon)	Commercial(Amazon)
Data storage	Solid-state drive (SSD)	Magnetic disk
Secondary indexes	Yes	No
Accessing method	API call	HTTP web address (API + publicly accessible URL)
Server-side script	No	No
Composite key support	Yes	No
Data consistency	Yes	Yes
Distributed counters	Yes	No
Largest value supported per item	64 KB	5 TB

DynamoDB versus Redis

Both DynamoDB and Redis are NoSQL databases that store the data in key-value format. But Redis is an open source database provided by BSD. **Redis** means **Remote Dictionary Server**. It is often called a data structure server as its key contains many data types, such as string hashes, in which the key and values are string, sorted sets of strings, stored sets, and lists of strings. We can perform atomic operations in Redis. Redis stores the whole dataset in memory, so we can persist it by dumping the data to disk, because Redis synchronizes data to the disk every 2 seconds. So if the system fails, we lose the data for only a few seconds. Another way to persist it is by appending each command to the log.

Redis supports master-slave replication, which allows the slave Redis server to be the same copy of the master Redis server with non-blocking replication. On the master-side server, it will handle queries when one or more slaves perform initial synchronization. On the other side, while the slave server performs initial synchronization, it will still handle queries using the old dataset. But in DynamoDB, replication is done at a scheduled time; a continuous data replication is not performed. So in this case, if a primary DynamoDB table loses its data, there can be data loss while restoring from the backups. In Redis, slaves, are able to accept connections from several slaves apart from slaves from the same master server. But in DynamoDB, the tables should be on the same AWS account.

Other features of Redis include transactions, pub/sub, Lua scripting capabilities, keys with a restricted time to live, and other configuration settings, which will allow Redis to work like a cache. Redis is written in ANSI C and works in almost all operating systems, such as Linux, BSD, and OS X without any external dependencies.

While data durability is not the major concern, the in-memory environment of Redis allows it to perform extremely well compared to database systems that write every update or change to disk before allowing a committed transaction. There is no prominent speed difference between read and write IOs. Redis works as a single process and is single-threaded. Hence a single Redis instance cannot apply parallel execution of tasks such as stored procedures. Redis is mainly used for rapidly changing data with a predictable database size that should mostly fit in-memory. So Redis is used in real-time applications such as storing real-time stock prices, real-time communication, real-time analytics, and leaderboards. We can use it as an option for memory cache too. Let's move on to the tabular comparison between these databases, as follows:

Specification	DynamoDB	Redis
Data model	Key-value store	Key-value store
Operating system	Cross platform (hosted)	BSD
		Linux
		OS X
		Solaris
Programming language	Ruby	C
License	Commercial (Amazon)	Open source with BSD-license
Data storage	Solid-state drive (SSD)	In-memory dataset (RAM)
Secondary indexes	Yes	No
Accessing method	RESTful HTTP API call	API call
		Lua
Server-side script	No	Lua
Triggers	No	No
Partitioning	Sharding	None
MapReduce	No (can be done with other services of AWS)	No
Composite key support	Yes	No
Atomicity	Yes	Yes
Data consistency	Yes	Yes
Isolation	Yes	Yes

Specification	DynamoDB	Redis
Durability	Yes	Yes
Transactions	No	Optimistic locking
Concurrency control	ACID	Locks
Partition tolerance	No	Yes
Persistence	No	Yes
High availability	Yes	No
Referential integrity	No	No
Revision control	Yes	No
Function-based index	Yes	No
Full text search	No	No
Geospatial indexes	No	No
Horizontal scalability	Yes	Yes
Replication method	Master-slave replica (asynchronized)	Master-slave replica (synchronized)
Largest value supported	64 KB	512 MB
Object-relational mapping	No	Yes
Log support	No	Yes
Operations per second	1000	140000
Free for commercial use	No	Yes (Up to some memory usage)
Deployment policy	Only with AWS	On premises
Easy to use	No	Yes
Backup	Scheduled (to configure)	Autosync frequently
User concepts	Access rights for users and roles can be defined via the **AWS Identity and Access Management (IAM)**	A very simple password-based access control
Best use	Rapidly varying data, frequently written, rarely read statistical data	Large to small database solution

So as per the previous comparisons, you can easily identify the most suitable NoSQL data service to work with your dynamic applications. In short, it provides the following features on the Amazon-distributed infrastructure and robust platform:

- Seamless scaling
- Secondary indexes
- Schema-less
- Strong consistency, atomic counters
- Integrated monitoring
- Secure
- Elastic MapReduce and Redshift, and data-pipeline integration
- Management console and APIs

Index

Symbols

A

B

C

D

E

F

G

H

I

Q

R

S

T

U

V

W

X

About Packt Publishing

Packt, pronounced 'packed', published its first book "*Mastering phpMyAdmin for Effective MySQL Management*" in April 2004 and subsequently continued to specialize in publishing highly focused books on specific technologies and solutions.

Our books and publications share the experiences of your fellow IT professionals in adapting and customizing today's systems, applications, and frameworks. Our solution based books give you the knowledge and power to customize the software and technologies you're using to get the job done. Packt books are more specific and less general than the IT books you have seen in the past. Our unique business model allows us to bring you more focused information, giving you more of what you need to know, and less of what you don't.

Packt is a modern, yet unique publishing company, which focuses on producing quality, cutting-edge books for communities of developers, administrators, and newbies alike. For more information, please visit our website: `www.packtpub.com`.

Writing for Packt

We welcome all inquiries from people who are interested in authoring. Book proposals should be sent to `author@packtpub.com`. If your book idea is still at an early stage and you would like to discuss it first before writing a formal book proposal, contact us; one of our commissioning editors will get in touch with you.

We're not just looking for published authors; if you have strong technical skills but no writing experience, our experienced editors can help you develop a writing career, or simply get some additional reward for your expertise.

Talend for Big Data

ISBN: 978-1-78216-949-9 Paperback: 96 pages

Access, transform, and integrate data using Talend's open source, extensible tools

1. Write complex processing job codes easily with the help of clear and step-by-step instructions.
2. Compare, filter, evaluate, and group vast quantities of data using Hadoop Pig.
3. Explore and perform HDFS and RDBMS integration with the Sqoop component.

Big Data Analytics with R and Hadoop

ISBN: 978-1-78216-328-2 Paperback: 238 pages

Set up an integrated infrastructure of R and Hadoop to turn your data analytics into Big Data analytics

1. Write Hadoop MapReduce within R.
2. Learn data analytics with R and the Hadoop platform.
3. Handle HDFS data within R.
4. Understand Hadoop streaming with R.
5. Encode and enrich datasets into R.

Please check **www.PacktPub.com** for information on our titles

Printed in Great Britain
by Amazon